CULTURE IN LANGUAGE LEARNING

CULTURE IN LANGUAGE LEARNING

Edited by

HANNE LETH ANDERSEN

KAREN LUND

KAREN RISAGER

 AARHUS UNIVERSITY PRESS

AARHUS UNIVERSITY PRESS
Langelandsgade 177
8200 Aarhus N
Denmark
Fax (+ 45) 8942 5380

White Cross Mills,
Hightown
Lancaster,
LA1 4XS
United Kingdom
Fax: 01524 63232

P.O. Box 511
Oakville, CT 06779
USA
Fax: 860-945 9468

www.unipress.dk

The editors gratefully acknowledge the financial support of the Aarhus
University Research Foundation and the Danish Language and Culture
Network

Contents

Introduction

Hanne Leth Andersen, Karen Lund and Karen Risager

This publication is the result of a conference held in Copenhagen on 18th May 2004 entitled 'Culture in Language Learning'. It was organized within the framework of the Danish Language and Culture Network, which was founded in September 2002 with the aim of establishing and encouraging a discussion of the goals, visions and objects of foreign language studies in Denmark, and covers a whole range of interrelated disciplines and subdisciplines such as language, literature, culture, society, history and learning. The network has given rise to a series of conferences and conference publications including Hansen 2002 and Hansen 2004. A focal point in the discussions has been to develop a more integrated view of foreign language studies than has traditionally been the case.

This volume seeks to explore these disciplines and subdisciplines from a language perspective by asking questions such as: In what ways is culture a part of language and of language learning and teaching? What does it mean to learn and teach a foreign (or second) language in the world of today?

Classical and modern language studies have always focused on language and culture in a wider historical perspective. In the national philologies, literature and other texts written in the national language were considered to be the clear and well-defined object of study, and the national-historical framework was generally not questioned.

With the increased focus on internationalization, globalization and post-colonial studies, languages and cultures can no longer only be associated with nations and national identities. They should also be associated with transnational processes, networks and communities. Languages and cultures are variably related to specific subjectivities and historicities, in particular due to exchanges between countries for various purposes such as studying, international careers, or personal relations across borders. Consequently, new approaches to foreign language studies are being developed and must be developed, taking their theoretical and methodological points of departure in new research fields such as culture studies, anthropology, sociology, communication studies, discourse analysis, text grammar and pragmatics. Simultaneously, the view of culture is changing from the traditional or classical view of culture as synonymous with art and literature, and representing the national patrimony, into a view that includes the various ways of life of the members of the target language community within or across national borders. This development implies that the aim of foreign language education can no longer be to enable the students to take over the specific foreign national identity, to become native speakers linguistically and culturally. The approach to languages and cultures today, especially at university level, is less normative, more open to variation, more communicative, and includes an interest in language and cultural encounters. Language teaching has to seriously take into account the fact that the languages being taught are foreign languages and that the goal of teaching is not to become 'French' or 'Spanish' or 'German', but to be able to communicate with people who have more or less different cultural backgrounds and identities. Foreign language learning and teaching should not only focus on communicative competence in a national context but also on intercultural competencies in a complex, multicultural world.

In her article 'Culture in Language Teaching', Claire Kramsch sets out to survey how the cultural dimension of language studies has been defined, taught and researched, and how current interdisciplinary approaches try to integrate learners' historicities and subjectivities in language education as regards foreign, second and heritage languages. She distinguishes between a modernist perspective focusing on the idea of the homogeneous national and territorial culture, including humanistic (literature and the arts), sociolinguistic (everyday life, norms and conventions) and intercultural (coping with two cultures) approaches, and a postmodernist perspective focusing on culture as a more subjective, portable and variable concept linked to the individual's history in variable contexts of language use. Culture is thus seen as identity and as a way of belonging.

Karen Risager's contribution, 'Culture in Language: A Transnational View', is also based on a critique of the modernist perspective and presents an analysis of a concrete example of foreign language teaching in a transnational perspective. Language teaching is seen as a linguistic and cultural contact zone where linguistic and cultural currents meet and are transformed and then sent on in the global flow of meaning.

The analysis distinguishes between languaculture and discourse, i.e., two levels of culture in language. *Languaculture* is associated with a particular language and includes a range of dimensions (semantic/pragmatic, poetic and identity related). The concept of languaculture is seen as a bridge between the structure of language and the socially constituted idiolect of the subject. Discourses, on the other hand, are not necessarily bound to a particular language, but spread from language to language via processes of translation and other kinds of transformation.

Eva Westin's article 'Cultural and Historical Narrative in Native and Non-native Speaker Language' works with the narrative sequence as basic to both spoken and written language. It is used as a multitask resource in informal as well as formal interactions. She focusses on narratives on cultural and historical events in exolingual conversations in French. The article then discusses the differences between native and non-native speakers of French in the production of stories dealing with cultural and historical events, and finally considers what can be improved in a learning situation so that students get a better awareness of the narrative sequence, how to structure it and the purposes for which it can be used.

In her article 'The Awareness of Context in Second Language Acquisition Theories', Karen Lund takes a critical view of the predominant second language learning theories in order to analyse how SLA theories conceive of the learner and to profile the extent to which contextual factors are integrated in theory building. Lund builds on the assumption that second language acquisition takes place through participation and interaction with native and non-native speakers or writers of the target language, and that learning processes are influenced by the socio-cultural conditions of the historical time and space. To further the theoretical discussions, she presents an approach to language different from the linguistic approach dominating SLA theories, and finally she presents an ecological approach to second language acquisition and pedagogy which may constitute a promising perspective for the construction of second language acquisition theory.

In the article 'Authenticity and Textbook Dialogues', Hanne Leth Andersen compares the communicative goals and objectives of modern foreign language teaching with the way communication and interaction are presented in a representative selection of beginning French textbooks for Danish learners. She finds that textbooks often provide material emphasizing basic morphology and sentence structure rather than the structure of dialogue. Indeed, knowledge about the grammar of dialogue is provided within research fields like politeness theory, conversation analysis and discourse analysis, but this knowledge does not seem to have been sufficiently integrated into the teaching of modern languages or in frameworks for classroom interaction. She recommends that textbooks include more culturally authentic dialogues emphasizing specific rules of politeness for interaction, which are a perfect arena for observing culture in language.

Written from the point of view of an educational technologist with experience in both mother tongue and foreign language teaching, Francesco Caviglia's paper 'Film Dialogue as a Resource for Promoting Language Awareness' builds on the assumption that language learning requires authentic and culturally relevant material and discusses how film dialogue – which has become more easily accessible due to recent developments in technology – can be a powerful resource for helping adult learners build on their own pragmatic competence to develop a more mature understanding of language and communication.

BIBLIOGRAPHY

Hansen, Hans Lauge (ed.) 2002. *Changing Philologies. Contributions to the Redefinition of Foreign Language Studies in the Age of Globalisation*. Copenhagen: Museum Tusculanum Press.

Hansen, Hans Lauge (ed.) 2004. *Disciplines and Interdisciplinarity in Foreign Language Studies*. Copenhagen: Museum Tusculanum Press.

Culture in Language Teaching

Claire Kramsch

Abstract

Until World War II, culture used to be seen as the highly literate component of language study. In the seventies, it became synonymous with the way of life and everyday behaviors of members of speech communities. Nowadays it has become embroiled in the controversies associated with the politics of ethnic identity, religious affiliation and moral values. This paper first surveys how the cultural dimension of language study has been defined, taught and researched. It then reviews current interdisciplinary developments in the way culture is conceptualized and how it is now seen as integrating learners' historicities and subjectivities in language education.

1. CULTURE: AN INTEGRAL COMPONENT OF LANGUAGE TEACHING

Culture has always been an integral component of language teaching. Until World War II, culture used to be seen as the literate or humanities component of language study. After the war and following the communicative turn in language pedagogy, it became synonymous with the way of life and everyday behaviors of members of speech communities, bound together by common experiences, memories and aspirations. These communities were seen as grounded in the nation – the national context in which a national language was spoken by a homogeneous national citizenry. In the last ten years, this unitary conception of one language = one national culture has become problematic. National standard languages have come to be seen as arbitrary constructions of the 19th century nation states as much as the social and political institutions that constitute national cultures. At a time of growing economic and political globalization, when cultural encounters are increasingly mediated by information technologies, whose and what culture(s) should we teach: national, regional, or global culture? Urban or rural culture? High brow or popular culture? Oral, written or cyberculture? Gay culture? Marketing culture? And what disciplinary discourse should we draw upon to understand culture: cultural studies, anthropology, ethnography, sociology, education? To what extent is culture separable from power and ideology? The concept of culture has become in many respects politicized and embroiled in the controversies associated with the politics of ethnic identity, religious affiliation and moral values. Ethnic and regional cultures have been rallying points for the politics of identity and for ethnic claims by speakers of minority, heritage, regional, endangered languages. Religious affiliation has been turned into cultural affiliation, as in the controversy surrounding the headscarf for Muslim women in French public schools. And, given the sectarian meanings given to the term 'culture' in recent times, questions are being raised about the future of foreign language education in multicultural democracies.

When exploring these questions, various trends of thought become apparent, themselves manifestations of various cultures of nationalism or universalism that preexisted the advent of globalization and the Internet. I first survey how the cultural dimension of language study has been defined, taught and researched for the teaching of English and other languages in the United States and Europe. I then review current interdisciplinary developments in the way culture is conceptualized and how it is now seen as integrating learners' historicities and subjectivities in language education.

2. THE CULTURAL DIMENSIONS OF LANGUAGE STUDY

There are roughly two different ways of looking at culture in language study, depending on one's disciplinary and political orientation, and on whose interests are being served: the modernist and the post-modernist perspective. They both co-exist today in the same language departments at the same universities.

2.1 THE MODERNIST PERSPECTIVE

In the pedagogic imagination of most language teachers around the world, the term 'culture' is associated with the context in which the language is lived and spoken by its native speakers, themselves seen as a more or less homogeneous national community with age-old institutions, customs and way of life. Culture is seen either as a humanistic or as a sociolinguistic concept, with the concept of the intercultural, that characterizes the contact between people from different cultures, being of concern to researchers in communication studies and in education.

2.1.1 A humanistic concept

As a humanistic concept, culture is the product of a canonical print literacy acquired in school; it is synonymous with a general knowledge of literature and the arts. Also called 'big C' culture, it is the hallmark of the cultivated middle-class. Because it has been instrumental in building the nation-state during the 19th century, big C culture, as the national patrimony, has been promoted by the nation state and its institutions, e.g., schools and universities. It is the culture traditionally taught with standard national languages. Teaching about the history, the institutions, the literature and the arts of the target country embeds the target language in the reassuring continuity of a national community that gives it meaning and value. The fact that in the U.S. foreign languages are still taught for the most part in departments of foreign language and literature and that the curriculum for foreign language majors still puts a heavy emphasis on the study of literature is a reminder that language study was originally subservient to the interests of philologists and literary scholars. In the 1980s, with the advent of communicative language teaching, the humanistic concept of culture gave way to a more pragmatic concept of culture as way of life. But the prestige of big C culture has remained, if only as *lieux de mémoire* in Internet chatrooms named, for example, *Versailles, Madison Avenue* or *Piccadilly* – cultural icons of symbolic distinction.

2.1.2 A sociolinguistic concept

With the focus now on communication and interaction in social contexts, the most relevant concept of culture since the 1980s has been that of 'little c' culture, also called 'small cultures' (Holliday 1999) of everyday life. It includes the native speakers' ways of behaving, eating, talking, dwelling, their customs, their beliefs and values. Research in the 1980s was deeply interested in cross-cultural pragmatics and the sociolinguistic appropriateness of language use in its authentic cultural context. To study the way native speakers used their language for communicative purposes, the Herderian equation one language = one culture was maintained and teachers were enjoined to teach rules of sociolinguistic use the same way they taught rules of grammatical usage (see functional-notional syllabi of the 1970s), i.e., through modeling and role-playing. Even though it now related to the variety of native speakers' uses of language in everyday life, culture was seen as pretty monolithic, like the native speaker him/herself. Teaching culture has meant teaching the typical, sometimes stereotypical, behaviors, foods, celebrations and customs of the dominant group or of that group of native speakers that is the most salient or exotic to foreign eyes. Striking in this concept of culture is the maintenance of the focus on national characteristics and the lack of historical depth.

The sociolinguistic concept of culture takes on various forms depending on whether the language taught is a foreign, second, or heritage language. In foreign language (FL) classes taught outside of any direct contact with native speakers, culture is mostly of the practical, tourist kind with instructions on how to get things done in the target country. In second language (SL) classes taught in the target country or in native speaker run institutions abroad (e.g., British Council, Goethe Institut, Alliance Française), culture can also take the form of exposure to debates and issues of relevance to native speakers in the target country, or of discussions about living and working conditions for immigrants. In heritage language (HL) classes taught to native speakers who wish to connect with their ancestral roots, culture is the very *raison d'être* of language teaching. It is, not, however, without presenting major difficulties when the heritage community has either lost much of its original everyday culture (e.g., Native American languages, see Hinton 1994), or when its speakers belong to a community that historically no longer exists (e.g., Western Armenian or Yiddish). The teaching of culture in HL classes is very much linked to identity politics (Taylor 1994).

2.1.3 Intercultural education
The term 'intercultural' emerged in the eighties in the fields of intercultural education and intercultural communication. Both are part of an effort to increase dialogue and cooperation among members of different national cultures within a common European Union or within a global economy (for a review, see Kramsch 2001). Intercultural education as a component of a humanistic education is pursued with particular intensity in the Scandinavian countries (e.g., Hansen 2004a & b) and in Germany (for a review see Königs 2003).

In foreign language study, the concept of intercultural learning has emerged in recent years in Europe alongside the concept of communicative competence (e.g., Bausch et al. 1994, Byram & Fleming 1998, Zarate

2004); it characterizes a form of language learning that is less focused on approximating a native speaker linguistic or pragmatic norm than it is based on the subjective experience of the language learner engaged in the process of becoming bi- or multilingual and struggling with another language, culture and identity. The concept has been an object of controversy in Germany between discourse analysts (Edmondson & House 1998) and educational linguists (Hu 1999).

For Edmondson & House (1998), as for many researchers in pragmatics, conversation and discourse studies, entities like culture, power, identity are constructed across turns-at-talk and in the minute-by-minute negotiation of face, stance and footing. Since, in their view, communication is the *raison d'être* of language learning, language instruction should focus on the study of culture in discourse, i.e., the cross-cultural dimension of discourse pragmatics and the misunderstandings or successful understandings brought about by the discursive management of language itself. Language teachers should teach non-native speakers how to recognize and adopt the discursive behavior of the native speakers whose language they are learning, in order to find out ultimately how they think, what they value, and how they see the world. In short, foreign language instruction should focus on communicative competence and the cultural dimensions of discourse competence, not on intercultural competence.

Hu (1999) argues that the concept of culture as used by Edmondson & House is too restricted and essentialistic. To assume that 'German culture' speaks through the discourse of a speaker of standard German is an inappropriate assumption in our days of hybrid, changing, and conflicting cultures. For Hu, concepts like 'communication', 'language' and 'culture' cannot be taken at face value but must be problematized. Hence the usefulness of the term intercultural, that covers intra- as well as interlingual communication between people who don't share the same history, values, and worldviews. An intercultural pedagogy takes into account the students' culturally diverse representations, interpretations, expectations, memories, and identifications, that are, in turn, thematized, brought into the open through personal narratives and multilingual writings, and discussed openly in class. Hu's perspective on culture, like that of many educators working with immigrants, is close to the post-modernist perspective discussed below.

The German debate surrounding the notion of intercultural is emblematic of the problematic role that culture plays in language teaching at a time when national and other collective cultures are increasingly denationalized, deterritorialized, and are becoming more hybrid than ever. With the increased mobility of people and global markets, popular culture is shared by young people around the globe; with television and the Internet, attitudes and worldviews are no longer associated with geographical locations but interpenetrate one another in a myriad ways. Culture becomes a portable and variable concept, linked to historical stereotypes, personal memories and socialization patterns or *habitus* (Bourdieu 1991), that are activated by individual speakers in face-to-face interactions or Internet communication and are always subject to change, depending on the interlocutor, the topic, and the circumstances. This more variable notion of culture is nowhere more apparent than in the teaching of English as a foreign or second language.

2.2 THE POST-MODERNIST PERSPECTIVE

In the teaching of English as the language of immigration, global employment, and global transactions, culture has taken on a radically different flavor than in traditional language teaching. Culture, in the territorial, hierarchical sense given by the modernist conception of the term, has been seen as a handicap to individual mobility, entrepreneurship, and change associated with the mastery of English as a second or international language. Culture in the teaching of English has therefore been resignified as a post-modernist concept referring to Discourse, identity and power. This view of culture has influenced the teaching of other languages as well.

2.2.1 *Culture as Discourse*

Drawing from post-modern theories of the multiple, conflictual, changing subject of our post-structuralist times and from the 'dialogic turn' in cultural theory, culture has become equated with what James Gee calls 'Discourse' with a capital 'D', i.e., "ways of using language, of thinking, feeling, believing, valueing, and of acting that can be used to identify oneself as a member of a socially meaningful group or 'social network'" (Gee 1990: 143). Discourses, as identity kits, are inherently ideological, in the sense that they lead people to put forward certain ideas and values at the expense of others. Because they are the products of history, they are related to the distribution of social power and hierarchical structure in society. For example, the distribution of *tu* and *vous* in French everyday discourse reflects changes in social structure in various periods of French history. The *tu* of solidarity, that was common during the French revolution and the revolution of May '68, became generalized among students, army comrades and young adults in the democratic France of the seventies and eighties, but the hierarchical *vous* has recently surfaced again as a sign of distinction in the economically competitive France of the turn of the century.

This view of culture establishes a much closer link between language, thought, and culture than in the modernist conceptions (Kramsch 2004). Culture as Discourse introduces the notion that every utterance is embedded in asymmetrical relations of power between communication partners, that culture in the form of language is embodied history, and that the meaning of this history is constantly renegotiated through language. For example, there have been various terms to denote those who oppose existing political regimes. The French who opposed German occupation during World War II were called 'resistants' by the French, 'saboteurs' by the Germans; the Iraqis who oppose the American occupation are called 'insurgents' by the Americans, 'guerillas' or 'martyrs' by the Iraqis; in Guatemala opposition to the regime was led by 'rebels' if you were on the side of the government, 'freedom fighters' if you were on the side of the opposition. The use of one or the other term said something about the political leanings of a newspaper and its readers. By placing culture squarely in Discourse, post-modernists have linked an individual's membership in a culture to his/her social and political identity.

2.2.2 *Culture as identity*

For Norton, identity signifies "how people understand their relationship to the world, how that relationship is constructed across time and space, and how people understand their possibilities for the future" (Norton 1997: 410), which matches roughly Kramsch's definition of culture as "membership in a discourse community that shares a common social space and history, and common imaginings" (Kramsch 1998: 10), but with the emphasis placed on the individual rather than on the collective. Shifting the emphasis from culture to identity in language teaching dissociates the individual learner from the collective history of the group, it gives people agency and a sense of power by placing their destiny in their own hands. For example, one of the immigrant women studied by Norton was able to draw strength from her identity as a mother to stand up to her landlord in front of her children and counter his image of her as a helpless non-native speaker of English from Czechoslovakia.

Atkinson echoes Norton as he reassesses the notion of culture in TESOL, which, he claims, has been underexamined up to now. In his post-modernist view of culture, he suggests that 'language (learning and teaching) and culture are mutually implicated, but that 'culture is multiple and complex' (Atkinson 1999: 647). He further posits that 'social group membership and identity are multiple, contradictory, and dynamic' and that 'all humans are individuals', but, he adds, 'individuality is also cultural.' Despite some dissenting voices, Atkinson's view of culture represents the dominant view of many teachers of English around the world, as well as TESOL's global and multinational ideology. This view is well captured by Shirley Brice Heath:

> ... all those who would have social science be rid of [culture] agree that researchers can no longer see the concept as viable in a world of volatile, situated, and overlapping social identities. Apprehension about the term is evidenced by... 'lexical avoidance behavior' that puts in its place terms such as 'discourse', 'praxis', or 'habitus' (Heath 1997: 113, quoted in Atkinson 2000: 753).

Ultimately, the lesser importance given to culture in the teaching of ESL than in other foreign languages might just be part of an ideology that likes to think of English as a multinational, culture-free language, or lingua franca that speaks all cultures and none in particular, and that can be appropriated and owned by anyone to express their own local meanings. Each person is seen as the intersection of an infinite number of partially overlapping cultures (Atkinson 1999: 637). American pragmatism instinctively resists pigeonholing people according to where they come from and prefers to see alone standing individuals and cultures as "fluid, ever-changing, and nondeterministic", i.e., unimpeded by their history. This view also reflects a concern not to stereotype individuals and essentialize their national characteristics, for fear that culture might become political. But such an ideology risks mapping onto the rest of the world a culture of geographic and social mobility and of an individual pursuit of happiness that is itself political and quintessentially American.

CLAIRE KRAMSCH

2.2.3 Culture as the moral right to be heard and listened to

The paradox is that once a person has been stripped of her national culture and been made into a free-standing, rational, autonomous agent, the burden is on her to maintain her integrity and free will against the enormous pressure to conform to the will of the marketing industry, and the demands of the national political majority. Cameron (2000) shows some of the pervasive ways of talking and thinking in a global culture that fetishizes 'communication', 'partnership', 'options and opportunities', 'initiative' and 'entrepreneurship'. In the U.S., the nationalistic discourse of 'freedom', 'democracy' and 'homeland security' is equally constraining. Membership in a cultural group seems to be the only safeguard left against the domination of the market and the tyranny of the majority. Hence the growing demands for political recognition of individuals who define themselves not as free standing individuals, but as members of cultural groups characterized by race, ethnicity, gender, occupation, sexual preferences, regional affiliation etc.

A post-modernist perspective understands cultures to be in principle of equal worth, but in fact they are objects of moral and ideological struggle; hence the term 'culture wars' to denote the clash between different social and moral values that different cultures represent (Taylor 1994). For example, the current debate about the wearing of the Muslim scarf in French schools highlights the dilemma of the French educational system that needs to maintain the hard won separation of church and state while preserving the right of each individual to his/her own culture. The popularity of social and cultural theory among language educators (e.g., Luke 1996) shows how closely language is related to power in the teaching of culture in language study. Ultimately, the need to teach culture confronts the language teacher with a political dilemma, namely, how to teach cultural and moral difference without ignoring the incommensurable and even conflictual aspects of that difference. The increasingly polarized world we live in does not make the task of the language teacher any easier.

3. NEW WAYS OF INTEGRATING LANGUAGE, CULTURE, HISTORY AND IDENTITY

Culture is being reconceptualized to respond to the different needs of the learners of foreign, second and heritage languages. Citizens of nation states need to learn the languages of citizens of other nation states, or *foreign* languages, for reasons either of employment or of national security. New immigrants to industrialized countries need to be integrated into the host societies by learning the host language as a *second* language. Long time resident immigrants feel the need to learn the language of their ancestors as a *heritage* language in order to reconnect with their roots. In all three cases, culture is seen as the indispensable key to understanding speakers' verbal behaviors and worldviews and the way they position themselves vis-à-vis others both in history and in the social structure.

3.1 FOREIGN LANGUAGES

Among foreign languages, English occupies a special position by virtue of its world-wide spread. Within the European Union, English is taught in schools side by side with other foreign languages, but its value is different and so is its perceived usefulness. Although the teaching of English in European schools is still very much oriented toward British or American national culture, research on English as the lingua franca of continental Europe is gaining momentum (Seidlhofer 2003). This lingua franca is not necessarily a culture-free global English, but rather a supra-national European dialect that takes on the cultural specificities of each host culture.

In Europe, there is a boom of interest right now in the teaching of languages other than English. New avenues of research focus, as mentioned above, on the intercultural components of language learning but also on its ecological aspects (Fill & Mühlhäusler 2001) and on pluriculturalism as a dimension of plurilingualism (e.g., Zarate 2004, Busch 2004). This research draws heavily on insights from literary and cultural studies, sociolinguistics and pragmatics, anthropology, and from a long tradition of study abroad and student exchange. In Europe, language educators are particularly concerned about the effects of globalization and the weakening of national institutions on the teaching of foreign languages. Hans L. Hansen, a Humanities scholar from the University of Copenhagen, speaks for many when he says that foreign language teaching in an era of globalization (global market and global terrorism) means "reflecting theoretically upon the relation between entities like language, culture, identity, history and the self-knowledge and imaginary world pictures as they are represented in art and literature" (Hansen 2004a: 115). He envisages a new role for culture: "Foreign Language Studies must learn to conceive of culture as an open, multivoiced and dialogical interaction full of contradictions, rather than as the deterministic, homogeneous and closed structure that belonged to the era of the nation state" (Hansen 2004b: 9).

The current tensions between the creation of a European community geared to the global market and the europeanization of national communities geared to political national identities, are leading toward the creation of a "third sector", i.e., a European multilingual public sphere in the media and in professional life that includes national, regional and local languages, minority and migrant languages, sign languages. This multilingual sphere or "sprachenfreundliches Umfeld" (Busch 2004: 164) is meant to sensitize Europeans of all walks of life to cultural diversity and encourage them to embrace public multilingualism and multiculturalism, understood as "a corrective against the interests of the nation state and a global market economy" (ibid.: 289, my translation). This also prepares them for the eventual emergence of a multilingual political European identity. It includes the screening of foreign films with subtitles, the tolerance to untranslated code-switches in public statements, the symbolic use of untranslated languages in greetings, leave takings etc., the airing of bilingual TV programs like ARTE. It includes efforts by the Council of Europe to move from an emphasis on translation and linguistic diversity to efforts to develop a plurilingual education based on critical language awareness, plurilingual identity formation, and intercultural understanding. This entails a turn toward a more hermeneutic, reflexive, interpretive kind of teaching, in which 'text' can serve as a common ground: conversational texts, written texts, visual texts, not as objects of philological exegeses or structural analyses but as dialogically constructed culture in action.

In the U.S., by contrast, the foundational field of research for all foreign language education is still second language acquisition (SLA) research. It has traditionally drawn its data predominantly from ESL or the beginning levels of foreign language instruction. Because of its mostly psycholinguistic and sociocognitive concerns, SLA research has not had much to say about the teaching of culture in language classes, except perhaps regarding learners' motivation to acculturate into a target community of native speakers, as is the case with many ESL learners. SLA research has been less interested in studying the cultural benefits of study abroad than in exploring the uses of computer-mediated communication to learn about foreign cultures without going abroad

(Warschauer & Kern 2000). It has aligned foreign language research with linguistics and psychology rather than with anthropology or cultural studies. It has thus exacerbated the split between the social sciences and the humanities, between language teachers and literature/cultural studies scholars in language departments at American universities. In the current political climate, U.S. federal funding is given in priority to research on the psycho- and sociolinguistic aspects of advanced language competencies for intelligence gathering purposes in the languages declared necessary for national security. It is not primarily concerned about their cultural or historical aspects.

3.2 HERITAGE LANGUAGES, SECOND LANGUAGES

In American domestic affairs, there is a notable rise of interest in heritage languages for *social and cultural* purposes: Native American ancestral languages, master-apprentice programs (Hinton 1994), interest in Western Armenian, Yiddish, Spanish, Chinese, Vietnamese, Korean as heritage languages linked to vanished or distant cultures (Peyton et al 2001). This interest is in part an ecological concern for the preservation of endangered languages, in part a romantic need to reconnect with one's roots in the face of the impersonal forces of the market and of information technologies, in part a desire to exercise long-distance proselytism in one's country of origin (e.g., Cuba, Armenia, Vietnam). Yet, the issue of which culture to teach (Cuban culture or Cuban-American culture? North Vietnamese or South Vietnamese or Vietnamese-American culture?) when teaching Spanish or Vietnamese in the U.S. has not yet been addressed in the case of heritage languages, probably because it is a politically sensitive issue.

By contrast, teaching the national culture of the host country is part and parcel of the socialization of immigrants learning the language of the land as their second language. Until recently the pedagogy of English as a second language was unabashedly acculturationist, indeed, assimilationist. It taught immigrants mainstream middle-class American or British ways of speaking, thinking and behaving in everyday life. In view of the increasingly multicultural nature of industrialized societies and following post-modernist conceptions of culture, new research is being drawn upon to conceive of culture in the teaching of second languages to immigrants. Language memoirs and personal testimonies of bilingual/multilingual individuals offer rich insights into the transcultural identities and subjectivities of language learners (e.g., Pavlenko & Lantolf

CLAIRE KRAMSCH

2000). The notion of 'third place', first introduced by Kramsch 1993, captures the need to think of culture as a subjective, portable, entity, linked to an individual's history and his/her variable subject position in variable contexts of language use. As a way of giving meaning to one's life, it is not a place to belong to but *a way of* belonging.

3.3   RESIGNIFYING CULTURE AS HISTORICITY AND
       SUBJECTIVITY

The term 'culture' has come to cover a host of phenomena that mean different things to different people: literate tradition or high C culture, level of civilization, way of life, ethnic membership, country of origin, nationality, ideology, religious affiliation, moral values. It is difficult to find a common objective denominator. However, in our contentious times, 'culture' has retained a sense of the irreducible, the sacred, that touches the core of who we are – our history and our subjectivity. Culture is embodied history. Theoretical perspectives on the cultural dimension of language research have thus drawn their inspiration from feminist and post-structuralist theories of the subject (Weedon 1987, Bourdieu 1991), and from theories of language as social semiotic practice (Kramsch 2002), as historical intertextual practice (Hanks 2000), as institutional and ritual practice (Rampton 1995), as discursive and conversational practice (Moermann 1988), and as ideological practice (Cameron 2000). These theories provide fruitful ways of bridging the individual and the social in language use. They enable us to see culture as that precarious third place where our historical and subjective self gets constructed across utterances and turns-at-talk between the self we have just been and the self we might still become.

BIBLIOGRAPHY

Atkinson, D. 1999. 'TESOL and culture'. TESOL Quarterly, 33(4), 625-65.
Bausch, K.R., Herbert C. & H.-J. Krumm (eds.), 1994. *Interkulturelles Lernen im Fremdsprachenunterricht*. Tübingen: Narr.
Busch, B. 2004. *Sprachen im Disput. Medien und Offentlichkeit in multilingualen a Gesellschaften*. Klagenfurt: Drava.
Byram, M. & M. Fleming 1998. *Language Learning in Intercultural Perspective*. Cambridge: Cambridge University Press.
Cameron, D. 2000. *Good to talk? Living and working in a communication culture*. London: Sage.
Edmondson, W. & J. House 1998. 'Interkulturelles Lernen: ein überflüssiger Begriff'. *Zeitschrift für Fremdsprachenlernen*, 9(2), 161-188.

Fill, A. & P. Mühlhäusler (eds.) 2001. *The ecolinguistics reader*. London: Continuum.

Gee, J. 1990. *Social Linguistics and Literacies. Ideology in Discourses*. New York: The Falmer Press.

Hanks, W. 2000. *Intertexts. Writings on Language, utterance, and context*. New York: Rowman & Littlefield.

Hansen, H.L. 2004a. 'Towards a new philology of culture'. In Jensen, J.H.C. (ed.) *The Object of Study in the Humanities*. Copenhagen: Museum Tusculanum Press, 113-126.

Hansen, H.L. 2004b. 'Foreign Language Studies and Interdisciplinarity'. In Hans L. Hansen (ed.), *Disciplines and Interdisciplinarity in Foreign Language Studies*. Copenhagen: Museum Tusculanum Press, 7-20.

Hinton, L. 1994. *Flutes of Fire. Essays on California Indian languages*. Berkeley, CA: Heyday books.

Holliday, A. 1999. 'Small cultures'. *Applied Linguistics*, 20(2), 237-64.

Hu, A. 1999. 'Interkulturelles Lernen. Eine Auseinandersetzung mit der Kritik an einem umstrittenen Konzept'. *Zeitschrift für Fremdsprachenlernen*, 10(2), 277-303.

Königs, F. 2003. 'Teaching and learning foreign languages in Germany'. *Language Teaching*. October, 235-251.

Kramsch, C. 1993. *Context and culture in language teaching*. Oxford: Oxford University Press.

Kramsch, C. 1998. *Language and culture*. Oxford: Oxford University Press.

Kramsch, C. 2001. 'Intercultural communication'. In: R. Carter & D. Nunan (eds.). *The Cambridge Guide to TESOL*. Cambridge: Cambridge University Press, 201-206.

Kramsch, C. 2002. 'Language and culture: A social semiotic perspective'. *ADFL Bulletin*, 33(2), 8-15.

Kramsch, C. 2004. 'Language, Thought and Culture'. In: A. Davies & C. Elder (eds.), *The Handbook of Applied Linguistics*. Oxford: Blackwell, 235-61.

Luke, A. 1996. 'Genres of power? Literacy education and production of capital'. In: R. Hasan & G. Williams (eds.), *Literacy in Society*. London: Longman, 308-38.

Moermann, M. 1988. *Talking Culture. Ethnography and conversation analysis*. Philadelphia: University of Pennsylvania Press.

Norton, B. 1997. 'Language, identity and the ownership of English'. *TESOL Quarterly*, 31(3), 409-30.

Pavlenko, A. & Lantolf, J. 2000. 'Second language learning as participation and the (re)construction of selves'. In: J. Lantolf (ed.), *Sociocultural theory and second language learning*. Oxford: Oxford University Press, 155-178.

Peyton, J.K., D.A. Ranard, & S. McGinnis (eds.) 2001. *Heritage Languages in America: Preserving a national resource*. McHenry, IL: The Center for Applied Linguistics and Delta Systems.

Rampton, B. 1995. *Crossing. Language and Ethnicity among Adolescents*. London: Longman.

Seidlhofer, B. 2003. 'Closing a conceptual gap: the case for a description of English as a lingua franca'. *International Journal of Applied Linguistics*, 11(2), 133-158.

Taylor, C. 1994. *Multiculturalism. Examining the politics of recognition*. Princeton, NJ: Princeton University Press.

Warschauer, M. & R. Kern (eds.) 2000. *Network-based Language Teaching: Concepts and practice*. Cambridge: Cambridge University Press.

Zarate, G. (ed.) 2004. *Cultural mediation in language learning and teaching*. Strasbourg: Council of Europe.

Culture in Language: A Transnational View

Karen Risager

Abstract

Foreign language teaching and learning is an eminently transnational endeavour paradoxically marked by a national (or ethnic) paradigm stating that both language and culture are to be seen as nationally (or ethnically) delimited and inseparable. How can we make more visible the transnational character of foreign language teaching and learning? The paper will approach this issue from a combined sociolinguistic, discourse analytical and social anthropological angle, focussing on different kinds of linguistic and cultural flow in social networks of various ranges. I will distinguish between three kinds of language flow in the world: linguistic flow, languacultural flow, and discursive flow. And I will show, by way of an example, how foreign language teaching may be viewed as a contact zone where different kinds of flow merge, are transformed and – in the final resort – sent on in the global flow of meaning.

1. FOREIGN LANGUAGE TEACHING AS A LINGUISTIC AND CULTURAL CONTACT ZONE

In this article I shall try to demonstrate that foreign language teaching (and learning) is an eminently transnational endeavour even if it is still mostly characterized by a national (or ethnic) paradigm implying that language and culture are nationally (or ethnically) delimited and inseparable. I shall do this by analyzing a teaching vignette from a specific theoretical angle drawn from anthropological theory on transnational cultural flow. The vignette is inspired by a realised teaching sequence (Svensson 1998) – one which I have extended and adapted to my own purposes.[1] The title of the teaching vignette is *Tour de France*:

> *"Tour de France*
> In German lessons in Class 10 (the optional class for 16-17 year olds) in the Danish Folkeskole, the topic *Tour de France* has been chosen, based on a number of articles taken from German magazines. There are both

male and female students, most of them are Danish, and there is also a boy with an Iranian background and a girl with a Dutch background in the class. The teacher is a Danish woman. The teaching takes place in autumn 1996, after the summer in which the Danish rider Bjarne Riis won the race (he rode for the German *Telekom* team). The magazines have an overall German perspective, but there are also interviews with some of the riders, both German and other nationalities. The class works with text extracts and discusses them, mainly in German, and also sometimes in Danish. Some of the students prepare and perform certain role-play activities in German taken from the riders' (imagined) lives. Others write individual fictive extracts from 'a rider's diary'. A group is given the task of trying to make a German version of the Danish song 'Ten small cyclists'. The class also talks (in Danish) about differences in the use of the German and Danish past and present perfect tenses and how the forms are used in the students' texts of 'a rider's diary'." (Risager 2006: 19-20).

The relationship between 'German language' and 'German culture' is very complex in this case. The uses of German, Danish and other languages (Farsi, Dutch, loanwords from English and French) are mixed and exhibit a certain sociolinguistic variability. The topic *Tour de France* frames a range of discourses on cycling and international sports competitions in a national (French), continental (European) and global perspective ('the world's greatest bicycle race'). The teaching is carried out in a foreign language context, outside the German mother tongue area. In what sense can 'German language' and 'German culture' be said to be inseparable in this case?

Moreover, the teaching sequence must not be treated as an isolated field of practice. *Tour de France* is a part of the spread of language and culture in the world, among other things the spread of (specific uses of) German in the Danish context. Language teaching is a particular institutionally shaped learning space where linguistic, discursive and other cultural flows merge, are transformed and sent on in the global flow of meaning. The *Tour de France* sequence is a linguistic and cultural contact zone.

Each of those participating in the learning sequence *Tour de France* (including the teacher) has a unique life history when it comes to linguistic and cultural resources. They have all learned their first language, and possibly other languages, in certain social and cultural contexts, and their linguistic and cultural resources are an important part of their identity. With an individual perspective and horizon of understanding, each of them contributes to the work on language, culture and society as a – more or less – conscious aspect of work on developing language skills. The media-communicated representations of the *Tour de France* that they may happen to know constitute a horizon of understanding for that which takes place in the teaching. Thus, teaching is linked to other kinds of national and transnational cultural flows in society.

The teacher is an agent in the orchestration of this interaction between various life histories and horizons of understanding: Along with the students, she influences what types of linguistic and cultural flows gain access to the learning space, and how they are dealt with there. The teacher oversees pedagogically determined linguistic and cultural norms: the German language norm, norms of behaviour in certain social environments in German-speaking countries, etc., and she may handle this role in various ways. She also has more or less direct influence on how linguistic and other cultural flows are spread outside the learning space: via dissemination in the family and the local area, via use in work contexts, via the use of media, on trips abroad, etc. This instance of language teaching, then, plays a role in the cultural and linguistic globalization process.

This is intended to be a dynamic image of language teaching as a social and cultural practice. The metaphor of flow goes against the usually static image of 'the context' and emphasises the lines of connection between language teaching and the outside world. It is an image that indicates that language teaching is a kind of language policy and cultural policy, and that the teacher is an important agent in this context (cf. Byram and Risager 1999, Guilherme 2002).

Here I place the sequence in a global context mainly inspired by the approach described in Ulf Hannerz 1992: *Cultural Complexity. Studies in the Social Organization of Meaning*. Hannerz is a Swedish social anthropologist who has developed a macro-anthropological model of cultural flow in the world and the resulting local organization of diversity or complexity. He defines culture very broadly as meaning, and focuses on cultural flow through social networks of varying ranges, from interpersonal interaction at the micro-level to processes of communication, human mobility and commodity transport at higher levels – national, transnational, transcontinental and global. An example of cultural flow would be the routes taken by various musical genres and styles, and their mixing or fusion in cultural centres around the world.

This is a very general and inclusive concept of culture, and Hannerz does not, for example, deal with language and language flows as such. In my analysis below I shall distinguish between four kinds of cultural flow, where the first three are kinds of language flow, while the fourth comprises other kinds of cultural flow (material ways of living, food and drink, clothing, music, pictures, architecture etc.)

- linguistic flows
- languacultural flows
- discursive flows
- other cultural flows

2. LINGUISTIC FLOWS

2.1 LINGUISTIC FLOWS IN SOCIAL NETWORKS

The use of a specific language may be seen as an almost continuous flow (and change) in social networks of people and groups of people. These networks may be located physically in individuals acting together, or they may be located in virtual space as communication networks made possible by information technologies such as telephone, the Internet etc. These networks develop further through migration and language learning. Danish language, for example, spreads in social networks all over the world where there are Danish-speaking people as settlers, tourists, sojourners, students etc. People carry their Danish language resources with them into new cultural contexts and put them to use in perhaps new ways under the new circumstances. People around the world are learning Danish for instance in Scandinavian Departments, and thus the Danish language is spread to new individuals and new social networks. Seen in this light, many of the world's languages are spreading in large global networks, and most local communities exhibit a linguistic complexity resulting from the interaction (and struggle) of several languages (i.e. users of several languages).

2.2 LINGUISTIC FLOWS IN TOUR DE FRANCE

2.2.1 *The target language*

The target language, German, functions here as a foreign language and not a second language for the students. It is also a foreign language for the teacher. The teacher's version of German is influenced by her personal experiences with German speakers in Denmark and in social environments and localities in German-speaking countries. She has good knowledge of written German, especially parts of the literature and the press, while she has never, for example, read a periodical in German about computers, travels or sailing. She has her own personal idea of what the German language is all about.

Apart from the teacher's input, there is also input in this class in the form of German-language newspapers and magazines. Language teaching is a context where many highly different written texts are often used to provide an all-round insight into various ways of using the target language; preferably, so-called authentic texts that originate in a target country and have not been produced with language teaching in mind. In the *Tour de France* example, the class uses magazines produced in Germany, and the texts have (perhaps) been written by German journalists, for example on the basis of material from international news agencies. Their texts contain many different voices: there are interviews with cyclists (which may have been conducted in German or in English or in French?) and with other participants: organisers, doctors, sponsors from many countries, employed in certain cases by transnational firms.

To a varying degree the students have experience and practice in speaking German, and some of them probably have quite clear ideas as to what 'German' is. On the basis of this experience and the interaction in the class, the students develop their personal German interlanguage. The sequence would have looked quite different if the teacher had had German as her first language. It would also have looked different if the material had been written by students from a multicultural school in Berlin (but still about *Tour de France* and still with a 'German' perspective), or by French students at a school in southern France, as part of a transnational e-mail network and with a 'French' perspective.

The students, via their mutual interaction, probably influence each other's interlanguage. In most cases it is perhaps the teacher who is the model, but it can be some of the students, depending on the social relations in the class. Other students will perhaps be used as 'anti-models', and their peers might even think: 'I don't want to speak like that, at any rate'. In the linguistic networks in the class the students and the teacher make ongoing use of language as an identity marker (Le Page and Tabouret-Keller 1985).

2.2.2 First languages

In the class involved there are three first languages represented: Danish, Farsi and Dutch (or rather idiolects of these – idiolect meaning each person's unique configuration of linguistic resources). During the sequence, the mother tongue of the Danish students is strengthened in certain respects: for example, they learn about German grammar in Danish, they translate between Danish and German, their private and inner speech in Danish has a certain place in their German teaching – and naturally also if they have homework between lessons. From time to time, the class actually has to carry out comparisons between German and Danish, and it is not unusual for Danish to be used in the teaching from time to time if it is necessary for the content to be understood – this is underlined at several points in the Danish curriculum guidelines. They do not, however, take account of the fact that an explanation in Danish does not necessarily help those students who do not have Danish as a first language but as a second language.

The Iranian boy's Farsi can only find expression as private and inner speech, and only when he is working on his own. Farsi is important for him in his acquisition of German, but it is a hidden resource that does not become public in the class. The Dutch girl, on the other hand, can use various Dutch words and expressions in the class, and the teacher is interested in discussing them as they can be used to explain historical relations between German and Dutch.

2.2.3 Other languages

Other languages in this case are Danish as a second language, English as a foreign language and French as a foreign language.

By taking part in this German class the Dutch and Iranian students may have their Danish strengthened as a second language, but we do not know if the use of Danish has in fact made their learning of German more difficult, or even perhaps confused them – this might apply to the Iranian boy in particular, for whom Danish and German could appear fairy similar as regards grammatical structure and word formation. The possibility of using English in order to explain certain things, which in some cases can be relevant, would be virtually unthinkable in a German as a foreign language lesson.

English loan words are quite numerous in the German texts on *Tour de France*: 'team', 'power', 'sprint', etc., as well as French words: *étape*, *champion*, etc. The teacher points out some of the English loan words, but not the French ones. She could possibly have asked the Iranian student to look for German loan words in Farsi.

2.2.4 Code-switching

Language teaching is mainly presented as being the teaching of a single language in curriculum guidelines, and in most academic literature. The object of teaching is the 'target language', and the fact that those taking part use their eventual common language (here: Danish as first and second language) from time to time is seen as a necessary evil – or maybe as a positive chance to develop students' language awareness. But language teaching is always bilingual or multilingual. It is precisely characteristic for this context that there is always at least one other language 'present'. Even when all teaching is carried out in the target language, the first language still exists in the students' universe and they use it, if nowhere else, in their private and inner speech while they are acquiring the target language. In addition, there will be some degree of language transfer from the first language – and possibly other languages the student may happen to know – to the target language.

Language learning can thus to a greater or lesser extent include constant code-switching (or code-mixing) between two or more languages. They can occur directly as translations in the class, but may also be in the form of communicative strategies where the first language and other languages are included in order to make the meaning clearer. There is a kind of code-switching in inner speech, as for example: 'I wonder what "issue" means here?' (said in Danish, for example). A foreign language class can prove to be a good example of a relatively compact bilingual or multilingual network in which experiments are made in creating bilingual or multilingual speech, for example conversations in German and Danish about cycling, with the use of such expressions as *das Gelbe Tricot*, which invites comparisons with the Danish *den gule trøje*, English 'the yellow jersey' and (perhaps) the French *le maillot jaune*.

It would be interesting to study the code-switching of language teaching using Le Page og Tabouret-Keller's theory of linguistic acts of identity (Le Page and Tabouret-Keller 1985). What kind of linguistic identity constructions take place when the teacher and the students switch between target language and first or second language? The switch is most often based on practical considerations to do with intelligibility and level of formulation, but identification is also included – with regard to national identities or group identities in the class, for example.

What kind of identity does language teaching try to establish? What does it mean to identify oneself with 'the target language' – i.e. those who speak this language?

A research tradition is developing that focuses on multilingualism in second language teaching – see, for example, Bourne 1988. Efforts are also being made to develop a didactics of multilingualism, especially in Germany (*Mehrsprachigkeitsdidaktik*), a didactics that to a greater or lesser extent attempts to develop awareness of the multilingual society and the multilingual class in foreign and second language teaching (Nieweler 2001, Oomen-Welke 2000).

3. LANGUACULTURAL FLOWS
3.1 THE CONCEPT OF LANGUACULTURE

The above description of linguistic flows has implicitly focused on the expression side of language (in the Saussurean and Hjelmslevian sense) or the code: It is codes that are seen as flowing and intermingling in social networks – irrespective of the meanings to which they give rise. With the concept of languaculture, the focus switches to the content or meaning side of language: What are the pragmatic, semantic and social meanings carried and constructed by the language in question (i.e. the users of the language)?

The American anthropologist Michael Agar has used the concept of languaculture in, for example, Agar 1994, and I have developed it further in Risager 2003, Risager 2004 and Risager 2006. I suggest that the concept of languaculture should be seen as covering three inter-related dimensions:

- the semantics and pragmatics of language
- the poetics of language
- the identity dimension of language

3.1.1 *The semantics and pragmatics of language*

The semantics and pragmatics of language is the dimension specifically explored by Agar, and by many others interested in contrastive and intercultural semantics and pragmatics. It has also been a longstanding focus of interest for linguistic anthropology since Boas, Sapir and Whorf. This dimension is about constancy and variability in the semantics and pragmatics of specific languages: It could be more or less obligatory dis-

KAREN RISAGER

tinctions between 'sister' and 'brother', between 'he' and 'she', between 'red' and 'orange', between 'hello' and 'how are you', between 'nature' and 'culture' etc. – and the social and personal variability that is found in concrete situations of use. This dimension thus has to do with the interplay of constancy and variability in the semantic potential of the language, for example the lexicon and metaphorical systems, and with the interplay of constancy and variability in the pragmatic potential of the language, for example politeness relations and rituals, the uses of indirectness, humour and irony etc.

3.1.2 The poetics of language

The poetics of language is the dimension related to the kinds of meaning created in the exploitation of the syllabic and phonological structure of the language in question – rhymes, relationships between speech and writing etc. – areas that have interested literary theorists focussing on literary poetics, style and the like.

3.1.3 The identity dimension of language

The identity dimension is also called social meaning by some sociolinguists, for example Hymes. It is related to the social variation of the language in question: in using the language in a specific way, with a specific accent for instance, you identify yourself and make it possible for others to identify you according to their background knowledge and attitudes. Linguistic practice is a continuing series of 'acts of identity' (Le Page and Tabouret-Keller 1985) where people project their own understanding of the world onto the interlocutors and consciously or unconsciously invite them to react. The identity dimension has been explored by those scholars within sociolinguistics that are interested in the relationship between language and identity in multilingual society.

3.1.4 Reasons for the introduction of the languaculture concept

There are two main reasons why the concept of languaculture is useful in the context of language and culture teaching and learning:

Firstly it offers an escape from the overall conviction that language and 'the rest of culture' are coterminous and inseparable. On the one hand, the concept stresses that no language is languaculturally neutral: all languages have specific cultural (meaning) dimensions such as the above-mentioned dimensions of languaculture. On the other hand, the concept also implies that it is not the case that every language is associated with 'a whole culture' – whatever that is. There are many kinds of culture that are not dependent on language although one can of course refer to them by means of language. Not everything cultural is linguistic, to put it briefly. Cultural practices, and cultural communities, are complex and changing (in a state of flow), and may cut across other communities such as language communities (Hannerz 1992).

Secondly, the concept of languaculture offers the opportunity of seeing foreign or second language learners, especially adults, as people who exploit their first language languaculture in the process of learning a new language. So, for example, when I start learning Italian, I have to use my Danish languaculture in the process of giving meaning to Italian words and expressions, and only much later will I be able to construct meanings that approximate those of what I imagine to be model native speakers. In learning Italian, I thus contribute to the spread of Danish languaculture in the use of a new code.

3.1.5 Linguistic practice and linguistic resources
The concept of languaculture applies both when we look at language as a dynamic and changing linguistic practice in social networks of various ranges, and when we look at language as resources developing in the individual subject. These two 'loci' of language are dependent on each other.

3.1.6 Languaculture in linguistic practice
If we consider languaculture in linguistic practice, oral or written, there is usually a high degree of semantic and pragmatic variability in the process. When a text is produced, languacultural intentions are laid down in the text, i.e. intentions concerning how this text is going to function semantically and pragmatically in that specific communicative activity: What speech acts are intended? What references are given? What representations of the world are created? These languacultural intentions are restricted or expanded in the course of reception of the text. The addressees or the readers interpret the text according to their personal languacultures and their knowledge of the world.

In situations where the language is used as a foreign language, there are many opportunities of adding even more variability to the text or communication than is the case with native language use: for instance as it is described by Agar in his comments on examples of intercultural communication in English between Austrians and himself (Agar 1994, Risager 2003).

3.1.7 Languaculture in linguistic resources

The personal languaculture of the individual cannot be separated from his or her personal life history and identity formation.

As for the case where the language is first language, it should be noted that the idea of an intimate relationship between language and culture primarily refers to the language in its function as a first language, even if this is rarely explicitly stated. The national-romantic idea of an inner association between the language and the people (the nation) is in fact about the people who have from childhood grown up with the mother tongue and the mother tongue culture (in German: *die mut-tersprachliche Kultur*).

This idea of intimate association between mother tongue and mother tongue culture at the national (or ethnic) level ignores the possibility of great variability in the linguistic and cultural upbringing of different individuals. The acquisition process is, in any case, socially differenti-ated; all human beings develop their personal linguistic and cultural repertoires. Therefore language and culture are always different from individual to individual, characterized by a specific perspective and a specific horizon of understanding. For example, the meaning of such notions as 'work', 'leisure' and 'rest' may be quite different even within the same professional group or the same family.

When the language in question is a foreign language, the relationship between language and culture is different. Analogously to what I men-tioned above, a Dane who is learning German, for instance, especially in the first stages of learning, must draw on his/her cultural and social experience related to the Danish language. There are some semantic/pragmatic distinctions that are obligatory in using German, such as an appropriate distribution of 'du' and 'Sie'. But besides such clear-cut dis-tinctions it will be natural to use the languaculture developed in relation to the first language (or other languages learnt). Personal connotations to words and phrases will be transferred, and a kind of language mixture will result, where the foreign language is supplied with languacultural matter from another language (in this case Danish, and possibly other languages learnt). From the learner's perspective, the alleged intimate association between German language and culture is normative, not descriptive. The learner's task is to establish an association between his/her language and his/her cultural experience, and this task has to be accomplished on the basis of a growing understanding of some of the associations (experiences, knowledge etc.) common among native speakers. But even when the learner reaches a high level of competence, his/her languaculture will always be the result of an accumulation of experiences during his/her entire life history, some of which has taken place outside the target language community.

Languaculture, thus, is both structurally constrained and socially and personally variable. It is a bridge between the structure of language and the socially constituted personal idiolect. The most interesting potentials of the concept may lie in the study of the personal idiolect with a focus on individual (but not necessarily idiosyncratic) semantic connotations and language learning as a process that is integrated in the life history of the individual subject, as a speaker-hearer, a reader and a writer.

3.2 LANGUACULTURAL FLOWS IN TOUR DE FRANCE

3.2.1 Semantics and pragmatics

Although the target language is German, several non-German languacultural practices may characterize the work in the class. Connotations of words such as cyclist (*Fahrradfahrer*) and France (*Frankreich*) may be more Danish (or Farsi or Dutch) than German. Each participant has his/her personal connotations to France, developed as a result of his/her own biography and experiences. The use of German is to some extent the use of a code with languacultural elements coming from other languages. One can say that the German language is spreading in the Danish context and at the same time incorporating languacultural elements from other languages in the specific contact zone of language teaching. These varieties of German (Danish German, Danish-Farsi German, Danish-Dutch German) may spread outside the school context and contribute further to the international variability of the German language.

3.2.2 Poetics

The students of the class are given the task of translating the Danish children's song *Ti små cyklister* (Ten small cyclists) into German (*Zehn kleine Fahrradfahrer*) and of singing it afterwards. The song has ten verses. In each of them one of the small cyclists makes a stupid mistake in the traffic and is 'out'. Finally, there is only one cyclist left and the last line says '*han kørte helt korrekt, så ham kan vi li'* (*Er fuhr nach allen Regeln, den mögen wir also gern*) (He rode his bike correctly, so him we like). This translation task is quite difficult, and it demonstrates a number of translation problems to do with the meaning of words and expressions as well as with the possibility of transferring rhythm and rhyme. Students encounter some of the different poetic potentials of the German and the Danish language. They may also suspect that this song has similar versions in other languages – maybe also in Dutch and Farsi.

3.2.3 Linguistic identity

The work with German in this class is influenced by the dominating Danish attitude to German, namely that it is a difficult language. German teaching often requires extra work by the teacher to create the sufficient learning motivation. The Danish attitude is to some extent shared by the girl with Dutch background, but not by the boy with an Iranian background. These differences in attitude are of course related to geopolitical history, among others the difficult historical relationship between Denmark and Germany. So the spread of German to this class carries with it a certain negative identity towards the language, even if the teacher does everything she can to avoid it. During the work with a translation, for instance, students come up with certain ideas of rules, control and punishment which they had not thought of in connection with the Danish version.

4. DISCURSIVE FLOWS
4.1 DISCOURSE AND DOUBLE INTERTEXTUALITY

Discourse, in the sense given to this term by critical discourse analysts such as Fairclough 1992, is content-oriented. It carries and forms themes, positions and perspectives. It is mainly linguistically formed (though often incorporated in wider semiotic practices), but it is normally not restricted to any specific language or language community. This means that discourses may carry content from one language community or network to another. Discourses may spread from language to language by processes of translation and other kinds of transformation. Discourses on nationalism, on agriculture, on Islam, on education, on culture, etc. etc. spread transnationally all over the world. But any discourse is at any time embodied in a specific language, and consequently formed by the languacultural potential of that language.

This means that in every text analysis and analysis of discursive practice one must adopt an intertextual perspective that is double: the text is always a meeting-place between two kinds of flow: linguistic flow (the flow of a particular language, such as Danish) and discursive flow (the flow of a particular discourse, such as nationalist discourse, or some other theme or fragment of a theme). The concept of intertextuality has to be analysed in these two highly different yet mutually connected forms. In every communicative event, languaculture(s) and discourse(s) are merged together and very difficult to disentangle, if not by way of translation (Risager 2003, Risager 2006).

4.2 DISCURSIVE FLOWS IN TOUR DE FRANCE

Discourses on cyclism, sport, professionalism and competitions are not particularly Danish, nor German. They do not circulate only in the Danish language community/network, or in the German community/network. They are transnational. They are channelled in a structured way in the global communication systems and may be assumed to be mediated more often in some languages than in others. In the *Tour de France* sequence, we see these discourses spread through German magazines and by the teacher in the Danish school context where they are reproduced and transformed in both oral and written language in German and Danish. Many personal perspectives are included though the overall perspective is Danish.

5. OTHER CULTURAL FLOWS

'Other cultural flows' covers a whole range of non-verbal cultural flows: visual, architectural, musical and behavioral flows, the spread of social structures and relations, etc.). Of course, all these different kinds of cultural flow take more or less different routes in the world, a topic I cannot deal with here. But the point is that cultural flow is complex and often transnational and global in character. This is an image of culture that is totally at odds with the static image of the national culture which is so often referred to in popular (and sometimes professional) discourse on language and culture teaching.

Cultural flow (in the inclusive sense used by Hannerz) is socially organized and influenced by power relations. In the study of cultural flow, Hannerz proposes to distinguish between the following four frameworks of social organization (Hannerz 1992):

- The framework of life forms organizes cultural flow in everyday life and interactions, characterized by local social relations and structures.
- The framework of the market forms and distributes cultural flow in local, national and transnational structures of commodity production, transport, advertizing and consumption.
- The framework of the state mainly circulates cultural flow in the state apparati as management and control.
- The framework of social movements spreads cultural flow, new ideas and messages, nationally and transnationally.

The four frameworks may be used to illuminate the character of the different kinds of language and cultural flow in *Tour de France*:

5.1.1 Life forms
The life forms find expression in the way the teacher and the students function during the short time they are together: how they interact linguistically in ways specific to the school as an institution, what languages they choose to use with each other both in the actual teaching situation and outside it. What subjects and points of view interest them separately as individuals – with a life also outside the school. How they position themselves spatially and socially in relation to each other and how they use their bodies, how they dress, whether they own a bicycle, etc. In the life-form framework, everyday life inside the classroom and at the school is connected to everyday life outside it, with a greater or lesser degree of continuity.

5.1.2 The market
The market mainly enters the teaching sequence in the form of the German newspapers and magazines that are used, i.e. the 'German perspective' of German public opinion is introduced in into the Danish German lesson. The students are thereby presented with certain

journalistic genres: reports, (reported) interviews, etc. The cultural representations contained in the material, both in text and images, help to provide the students with mirrors for their own lifestyles, perspectives, identities and images of the world. The walls of the German classroom are also decorated with postcards and posters showing the Austrian Alps, produced by the tourist industry in Austria and also mediated via the transnational market. The market framework communicates a virtually worldwide circuit of production, distribution and consumption of goods, and the class has been connected to this circuit via the teacher's purchase and use of the German printed matter.

5.1.3 The state

The state is present in many ways in the teaching sequence: The Danish state has laid down what objective status German is to have among the foreign languages on offer in the educational context involved. It has shaped the teacher's education and the teaching itself via executive orders, guidelines and examination requirements, etc. It has been responsible for the building and other material resources. The German class is part of the state bureaucratic hierarchy, and as such it is subject to both open control and allocation of resources.

5.1.4 Social movements

The social movements have provided impulses for the actual interaction in the class, e.g. norms and ideas about gender relations. This subject is also dealt with discursively in some of the material the teacher has brought along. She has, for example, found a brochure about the special *Women's Tour de France* and introduces this text in order to discuss the question of gender hierarchies in the world of sport.

6. CULTURE IN LANGUAGE: TWO LEVELS

The analysis of *Tour de France* reveals that there are two levels of culture in language: languaculture and discourse. Languaculture is related to one or more specific languages (Danish languaculture, Danish and German languacultures combined in the use of German as a foreign language), whereas discourse is generally not related to any specific language. Still, discourse (in the sense I am using it here) is always embodied in a specific language and marked by the languacultural potentials of that particular language.

The *Tour de France* example is untraditional but not unrealistic. It is of course easy to come up with examples of teaching sequences that focus to a greater extent on the target language and on issues more clearly related to the target language countries: It might be a sequence in English teaching in a Danish upper secondary school, for example, where both the students and the teacher all have Danish as their first language, where only English is spoken, where the work has to do with comprehending and discussing a short story about English conditions written by an Englishman who speaks English as his first language.

Or, even more focussed: It could be a sequence in Danish, as a second language, that takes place in Denmark where the teacher has Danish as her first language and the students come from various linguistic backgrounds but speak Danish exclusively. The work could be based on a Danish newspaper article that has been written by a journalist who has Danish as his first language, and which deals with a topic that is specifically Danish – for example the very large pork production in Denmark.

But even if language teaching is more focussed on issues closely related to one of the target language countries, it will always involve a multidimensional linguistic and cultural contact, one where gender, social class, life experiences and mastery of language will be able to play a role, and where a wide range of discourses and topics (fiction and non-fiction) are treated. We still lack ethnographically-oriented classroom research that takes *both* interaction in the class and the discursive content being dealt with into account. We need a truly interdisciplinary approach to language and culture teaching and learning that is based on a combination of sociolinguistics, discourse analysis and social anthropology. Such a theoretical combination may provide us with the necessary tools to illuminate the relationship between language and culture with a focus on the two levels of culture in language: *languaculture and discourse*.

NOTES

1 This brief analysis is based on the analyses in Risager 2003, and Risager 2006, which contain a much more elaborate examination of the relationship between language and culture from a cultural studies and global perspective.

BIBLIOGRAPHY

Agar, M. 1994. *Language Shock. Understanding the Culture of Conversation*. New York: William Morrow.

Byram, M. & K. Risager 1999. *Language Teachers, Politics and Cultures*. Clevedon: Multilingual Matters.

Bourne, J. 1988. '"Natural acquisition" and a "masked pedagogy"'. *Applied Linguistics*, 9 (1), 83-99.

Guilherme, M. 2002. *Critical Citizens for an Intercultural World. Foreign Language Education as Cultural Politics*. Clevedon: Multilingual Matters.

Fairclough, N. 1992. *Discourse and Social Change*. Cambridge: Polity Press.

Hannerz, U. 1992. *Cultural Complexity. Studies in the Social Organization of Meaning*. New York: Columbia University Press.

Le Page, R. & A. Tabouret-Keller 1985. *Acts of Identity: Creole-based Approaches to Language and Ethnicity*. Cambridge: Cambridge University Press.

Nieweler, A. 2001. 'Sprachübergreifend unterrichten. Französischunterricht im Rahmen einer Mehrsprachigkeitsdidaktik'. *Der fremdsprachliche Unterricht, Französisch* 1, 4-13.

Oomen-Welke, I. 2000. 'Umgang mit Vielsprachigkeit im Deutschunterricht – Sprachen wahrnehmen und sichtbar machen'. *Deutsch lernen* 2, 143-63.

Risager, K. 2003. *Det nationale dilemma i sprog- og kulturpædagogikken. Et studie i forholdet mellem sprog og kultur*. Copenhagen: Akademisk Forlag.

Risager, K. 2004. 'A social and cultural view of language'. In: Hans Lauge Hansen (ed.), *Disciplines and Interdisciplinarity in Foreign Language Studies*. Copenhagen: Museum Tusculanum Press, 21-34.

Risager, K. (2006). *Language and Culture. Global Flows and Local Complexity*. Clevedon: Multilingual Matters.

Svensson, I. 1998. 'Tour'en på tysk'. *Sprogforum* 10, 32-34.

Cultural and Historical Narrative in Native and Non-native Speaker Language

Eva Westin

Abstract

The narrative sequence is basic to language, both spoken and written, and is used as a multitask resource in familiar as well as formal interactions. In this article the narrative sequence is approached from a somewhat particular angle. I have chosen to focus on those narratives where the subjects concern cultural and histori-cal events in exolingual conversations in French. The article then discusses the differences between native and non-native speakers of French in the production of stories treating cultural and historical events. I also discuss what can be improved in a learning situation by students gaining a better awareness of the narrative sequence, how to structure it, and for what purposes it can be used.

1. INTRODUCTION

This article is based on one of the types of conversational narratives studied in my doctoral thesis (Westin 2003) which focuses on the types, forms and functions of the narrative sequence used in dialogue between native and non-native speakers of French. Why is the narrative sequence of such interest to language learning? Well, telling a story is something we all engage in very often in a situation of communication, and also a skill we learn at an early age. At the age of about nine we are capable not only to describe certain events in order of time, but also of foreground-ing them in relation to a background and of creating a plotline (Berman & Slobin 1994). At this age, then, we are able to produce an elaborate, cohesive and coherent story in our mother tongue(s) (van Dijk 1980). Being able to tell a story is therefore basic in human communication (Abbott 2002) and is used as a multitask resource in familiar as well as formal interactions. This is also the reason why the ability to produce and to identify narrative sequences, to tell a story and to understand one, is vital to students learning a second language.

2. BACKGROUND

In my thesis (Westin 2003) I have focused on the conversational narrative in the exolingual situation of French, i.e. in conversations in French between native and non-native speakers. The material (Corpus Westin) consists of 35 exo- and endolingual semi-spontaneous conversations each lasting around 30 minutes. Of these conversations 24 are exolingual in French, eight are endolingual in Swedish and three endolingual in French. As my interest was mainly concentrated on the exolingual aspect of the material and in particular the differences between Swedish learners of French and French native speakers, I analyzed the 24 exolingual conversations and as a reference also the three endolingual conversations in French. In these I found a total of 273 narrative sequences of which 189 were produced by a native speaker and 84 by a non-native speaker. The Swedish informants are students of French on different levels of university studies and the native speakers of French are students who have come to Sweden as exchange students within the ERASMUS program. See table 1:

NNS / NS	NNS Level A	NNS Level B	NNS Level C	NNS Level D
Félix Florence	Alf Ada Anne	Boo Bella Beatrice	Cissi Carin Cia	Dag Disa Daniella
Fabrice Françoise				

Table 1: Distribution of informants

My interest in the narrative sequence deepened as I realized that the speakers use the narrative a lot in simple as well as elaborate forms, for different purposes. The thesis compares structures of narratives produced by native and non-native speakers respectively, to see how the narratives are introduced in the flow of conversation, to apprehend their functions in the conversation and last, but not least to see what subjects are treated in the narratives.

As for the internal structure of the narrative sequence I have been able to see that neither native nor non-native speakers always use the entire narrative structure (abstract, orientation, development, complicating actions, evaluation, coda – see Adam 1984, Labov 1997 and,

2002, Revaz 1995, Norrby 1997), but that the structure is dependent of the conversational situation. This means that in a situation where all the constituents are needed they are also used; for example, the non-native speaker may need help from the native speaker to produce some parts of the constituents. Conversely, in a situation where some of the facultative constituents are superfluous, they are also omitted; for example, the abstract can be a part of the surrounding conversation, or the coda can be produced by the other speaker. What seems to be the most difficult task for the non-native speaker is to find the right words, to be able to maintain the narrative space and also to recognize a story told by the native speaker.

As far as the introduction of the narrative is concerned I have seen that it can be provoked or introduced by the narrator himself or by his narratee (récit auto- or hétéro-initié). The hetero-introduced narrative is often used by the non-native speakers, who tend to dominate on an interactional level, whilst the auto-introduced narrative is more frequently used by the native speakers, who normally dominate on a quantitative and topic related level. Depending on whether the speaker is native or non-native, the narrative is more or less continuous (récit continu or récit discontinu). The story may also be told by the speakers together (récit co-narré) or be produced as a direct response to a prior story told by the other speaker (récit en echo), where the principles of cooperation and reciprocity play an important role. I have also studied some cases of retold stories (récits en constellation) (Laforest 2001, Norrick 1998a, 1998b and 2000) where one story is told by the same narrator on different occasions to different narrates (narrataires).

The basic function of the narrative is always one of explaining things and helping the participants to approach each other. The story helps develop the relations between the individuals. Most of the narratives in my corpus serve as pure explanation, sometimes combined with an argumentative part for or against the question discussed. Only a few narratives with an anecdotal function were found.

3. CULTURAL AND HISTORICAL SUBJECTS IN NARRATION

And now to the main concern of this article, namely the topics evoked in the narratives and in particular the ones treating cultural and historical topics. Parallel to the study of structure, form and function the parameter of topic was an important matter. In my material I found three main types of topics: the private or personal, the cultural and the historical. The personal narrative implicates what we normally see as one of the main characteristics of a story, i.e. the fact that the speaker tells about an experience he himself has taken part in or witnessed. The personal narrative, then, is a story based on the narrator's own experiences and in my material the narratee has no knowledge of, or insight into, these experiences since the speakers only have superficial knowledge of each other. On the other hand, the cultural and historical narratives deal with events in which the narrator has not been neither active nor witness. Even though the narrator has not taken active part in the events, one of the speakers may be closer to the event than his interlocutor, depending on the cultural bonds between the story and the speaker's cultural membership, comparable to O-events "known generally to members of a group or a culture" (Norrick 2000: 106).

Apart from these general aspects that distinguish cultural and historical narratives from personal dittos there are some fundamental characteristics that distinguish the cultural narrative from the historical one. The cultural narrative treats topics recent in time, topics that are presented in the media and which often become shared knowledge on both the general and detailed level of information. Concerning the historical narrative, the topics treated are more distant in time, topics often learned in school or within the family. The general information is normally shared but the details of persons involved and of cultural specificities are not.

Let us compare the two following examples of which the first is a cultural narrative and the second an historical one.

Conversation exolingue – récit culturel: « deux jeunes étrangers tués »

(FLO = Florence, narrateur native; DAN = Daniella, narrataire non native) (R=Abstract, O=Orientation, E=Evaluation, D=Development, C=Complication, Ch=Coda)

*FLO oui non on en parle pas trop mais c'est-à-dire que le Front National fait tellement parler de lui euh par rapport aux actions qu'il mène (*DAN mm) {$_R$ je sais pas si t'as entendu parler qu'il y a euh euh y a deux ans je crois y a deux colleurs d'affiches du Front National qui ont tué un jeune maghrébin}

*DAN   hmm oui

*FLO   tu en as entendu parler

*DAN   euh ils l'ont jeté dans la Seine ou (#) c'est pas ça non

*FLO   euh c'est encore autre chose

*DAN   (rire) ah d'accord

*FLO   {$_O$ y en a eu deux(*DAN mm) en fait oui y a c'est non ce que y avait eu à ce moment là c'était qui y avait des y avait une mani-festation} / {$_E$ euh je sais plus pourquoi c'était} {$_D$ et y avait deux euh deux skinheads qui avaient jeté un euh un un maghrébin euh dans la Seine}

*DAN   hmm oui c'est ça

*FLO   {$_O$ mais ou euh un étranger je sais plus de quelle originéité il était mais ce que y a eu aussi c'est (bruit du magnétophone)

*DAN   oh là là

*ENS   (rire)

*FLO   mais ce qui y a eu aussi c'est qu'y a eu euh deux

*ENS   (rire)

*FLO   deux colleurs d'affiches du Front National euh} {$_D$ euh qui ont tué un jeune à coup de couteau je crois ou un truc comme ça ou ils avaient un pistolet} {$_E$ je sais plus / c'est c'est une autre histoire aussi}

*DAN   oui

*FLO   {$_C$ parce que là les deux qui ont jeté euh le la personne dans la Seine c'était pas des // si tu veux c'était des partisans du Front National mais eh ils ils soutenaient Le Pen quoi si tu veux (*DAN mm) mais ils faisaient rien / rien d'effectif pour lui tandis que là les deux qui ont tué le jeune maghrébin ils collaient des affiches donc ils travaillaient pour le Front National (*DAN mm)} {$_{Ch-E}$ donc ils étaient membres actifs (*DAN d'accord) et ça vraiment fait un tolet pas possible en France}

*DAN   je

*FLO   {$_O$ je crois que c'était même à Marseille que ça s'est passé}

In this dialogue Florence (FLO) is the native speaker and Daniella (DAN) the non-native speaker. When we enter the conversation they talk about crimes being committed by members of the National Front. This is a cultural narrative as it treats news that has been quite recently presented in both the Swedish and French press. As the subject is closely related to the French political climate, Florence is the one introducing the narration that she wants to transmit on this topic. What happens, however, is that Daniella responds directly but remembers a different occasion than the one to which Florence refers. The two events will then be told by Florence. Daniella takes active part but is not the one leading the narration. She gives the impression of following well but not knowing all the details.

Conversation exolingue – récit historique – « la guerre d'Algérie »
(FEL = Félix, narrateur natif; ADA = Ada, narrataire non native)
(R=Abstract, O=Orientation, E=Evaluation, D=Development, C=Complication, Ch=Coda)

*FEL hmm non $\{_R$ vous étiez neutres en plus donc ça ça ava avance pas les choses ça avantage pas les choses (*ADA non) euhm > c'est une période effectivement c'est un peu comme notre euh nous on a la guerre d'Algérie} $\{_O$ qu'on connaît pas / euh qui est toujours pas considéré comme une guerre officielle

*ADA c'est toujours comme ça euh

*FEL on en parle pas

*ADA qu'on ne connaît pas

*FEL on connaît très mal on vient de savoir} $\{_D$ on vient d'apprendre y a quoi y a un mois que combien y a eu de morts euh à une manif à une manifestation qu'il y eu en 61} (*ADA aha) $\{_O$ c'était Papon d'ailleurs le préfet de c'était le préfet de Paris} / $\{_D$ y a eu 38 morts je crois et on l'a on l'a su on a su y a quelques quelques années plus tard ou quelques mois plus tard qu'y avait eu des morts (*ADA mm) euh oh qu'y avait vraiment eu une boucherie (*ADA oui) et euh on sait maintenant qu'y aurait eu 38 morts} /

*ADA $\{_O$ et et c'était en quelle a quelle année

*FEL en 61 (*ADA 61)} $\{_C$ et y a beaucoup de choses comme ça euh qui qui sont pas très connues notamment euh ce qui s'est passé en Algérie} / $\{_R$ et c'est très intéressant d'écouter les témoignages des gens qui ont habité qui ont vécu en Algérie} $\{_O$ les pieds-noirs (*ADA mm) les gens qui ont été euh qui ont fait leur service militaire en Algérie qui ont été militaires (*ADA mm) où les les / les les enfants d'Algériens de de pieds-noirs (*ADA mm) ou les harkis (*ADA mm) les Algériens qui sont battus pour l'armée française et qui sont maintenant en France ils sont pas reconnus d'ailleurs} {_E c'est intéressant de les écouter} {_D parce qu'il y a il y a une histoire officielle à propos de de l'Algérie} / {_C euh y a des gens qui doivent avoir des choses à se reprocher un peu comme pendant la Seconde Guerre Mondiale où on attend qui meurent le plus pour euh pour euh vraiment euh dévoiler la vérité} > {_{Ch} y a un grand tabou à propos de la guerre d'Algérie

*ADA mais c'est toujours comme ça c'est

*FEL hmm et pendant cette guerre pendant la seconde guerre mondiale pareil il y avait un grand tabou}

The second example is an historical narrative in which Félix (FEL), native speaker, and Ada (ADA), non-native speaker, are involved in a discussion on the period of the World War II. Ada mentions that there are some facts about the Swedes and the war that have not been revealed or clarified. Félix then illustrates with a mirroring event from French history: i.e. that certain facts about the war in Algeria were first revealed many years after the war had ended. Ada produces an evaluative sequence at the end to confirm that the narrative sequence also illustrates the Swedish situation. The topic treated here is of course historical.

I have found many cultural and historical narratives in my corpus and the distribution between native and non-native speaker is presented in the following table (Table 2):

	Native speakers	Non-native speakers
Cultural narrative	78 (71%)	32 (29%)
Historical narrative	52 (93%)	4 (7%)

Table 2: Types of narratives

One of the reasons for the finding of so many cultural and historical narratives was that the speakers – in order to have a "lifeline" of topics – read some articles of current interest from *Le Nouvel Observateur* (a weekly French magazine) before they met. These articles treated cultural and historical subjects and often opened the way for other narratives of a cultural or historical kind. Another reason why private and personal subjects are less frequent is that the informants did not know each other prior to the recordings.

Compared to the personal narratives (107 in total, out of which 48 (45%) were produced by a non-native speaker and 59 (55%) were produced by a native speaker), the distribution of cultural and historical narratives is less equal between the two groups. An interesting fact is that it seems to be more complicated for the non-native speakers to produce a narrative sequence on a topic distant to themselves both in time and in space than to produce a narrative sequence of an event in which they themselves have been involved. This is why the distribution of personal narratives between native and non-native speakers is more equal than the distribution of cultural and historical ones. One reason is of course that, most probably, the speakers have told the same personal story before, if not in French (for the non-native speakers) then in their mother tongue. They also have direct knowledge, first hand information, of the story which gives them some security and, even more important, the narrative space.

The cultural narratives are more frequent with the native speakers and even more so, the historical ones. This difference in production is basically due to the difference in linguistic skills of the two groups. The non-native speakers have difficulties finding the correct words, they have difficulties remembering the words and expressions used in the articles where the vocabulary implicates more technical terms, institutions and facts related to society and history. Moreover the non-native speakers probably have difficulties in identifying with the ways in which journalists in the French magazine argue, describe and explain.

The fact that the speakers come from different cultures is also a reason for the difference in distribution. The articles taken from a French magazine give an advantage to the native speakers, both when it comes to language, structure and content. But in addition the non-native speakers also testify that the native speakers in general have a better knowledge of historical and cultural facts, something that adds to their linguistic disadvantage. When the knowledge about a cultural or historical event was shared by the two speakers, this story was co-narrated, something that shows the good intention of actively participating and cooperating from both the non-native and native speakers. Some of the historical narratives were also affected by a strong didactic contract depending on the native speaker's will to explain and the non-native speakers will to understand.

4.   WHAT CAN WE IMPROVE BY TEACHING?

I am convinced that an awareness of what a narrative sequence in conversation consists of is something critical to a language learner. Since the telling of stories in order to argue, explain and amuse is a frequently used conversational phenomenon, the students need to be able to recognize a narrative sequence in a foreign language. They need to recognize it in order to be able to give the correct feed back signals, to give the narrator his rightful narrative space and also to be able themselves to be creative in their second language. We know how to structure and tell a story in our mother tongue but are not aware of the difficulties we meet when we want to illustrate something with a story in a second language.

The importance of a rich vocabulary, the importance of knowing how to maintain a turn, how to win the interactional and narrative space and how to catch the interest of our next speaker are crucial to the dialogue. It is therefore very important for the students to enrich their vocabulary to cover areas less closely connected to themselves. A way of obtaining a richer vocabulary is, of course, to read, write and talk in class and with native speakers. When talking to native speakers the situation of telling stories to illustrate, argue and amuse will be of great importance and the students will learn in authentic conversation. Another way in which a larger vocabulary can be acquired is in dramatization of discussions and argumentation where material based on texts in the target language has been given to the students in advance. Concerning feedback signals, the students need to be able to control the small words, conversationally holding the meaning of the context and the purpose of the sequence, both when they produce and when they listen to a story in order to recognize and to give the right feed back. When it comes to cultural and historical knowledge it is of great importance that we explain and show to the students the differences between the mother tongue and the target language, both on a linguistic and a general level.

This shows that the ability to use a target language is concerned not only with the linguistic skills but also with a larger knowledge of the cultural and historical climate, both in our own country and in the countries where the target language is used. It is extremely important for the non-native speaker to be able to recognize a story and to be able to produce a narrative sequence in the conversational flow. It is also very important for the non-native speaker to have the capacity to use the story in different functions and to use correct vocabulary that is relevant to the topic. If a language learner is aware of all these things he can follow, produce and be creative in the conversational situation. If, furthermore, he has been introduced to and has become accustomed to the situation of using the narrative sequence, he has all the possibilities to develop in, and learn from, this situation.

BIBLIOGRAPHY

Abbott, H.P. 2002. *The Cambridge Introduction to Narrative*. Cambridge: Cambridge University Press.

Adam, J.-M. 1984. *Le Récit*. Paris: Presses Universitaires de France.

Adam, J.-M. 2001 (1997). *Les textes – types et prototypes*. Paris: Nathan Université.

Berman, R.A. and D.I. Slobin, 1994. *Relating Events in Narrative: A Crosslinguistic Developmental Study*. Hillsdale New Jersey: Lawrence Erlbaum Associates Publishers.

Bres, J. 1994. *La Narrativité*. Louvain-la-Neuve: Éditions Duculot.

Bres, J. 2001. 'De la textualité narrative en récit oral: l'enchaînement des propositions', *Revue Québécoise de Linguistique*, 29(1), 23-50.

Chafe, W. 1998. 'Things we learn from repeated tellings of the same experience'. *Narrative Inquiry*, 8, 269-285.

Kerbrat-Orecchioni, C. 2002. 'Les récits conversationnels, ou la parole 'ordinaire', c'est tout un art'. In: *Littérature orale, paroles vivantes et mouvantes*. Lyon: Presses Universitaires de Lyon, 99-121.

Labov, W. 1978. *Le parler ordinaire*. Paris: Minuit.

Labov, W. 1997. 'Some Further Steps in Narrative Analysis': http://www.ling.upenn.edu/~wlabov/home.html, (downloaded April 2002).

Labov, W. 2001. 'Uncovering the event structure of narrative': http://www.ling.upenn.edu/~wlabov/home.html, (downloaded April 2002).

Labov, W. 2002. 'Ordinary Events': http://www.ling.upenn.edu/~wlabov/home.html, (downloaded April 2002).

Labov, W. & J. Waletsky 1967. 'Narrative Analysis: oral versions of personal experience'. In: J. Helm (ed.), *Essays on the Verbal and Visual Arts*. Seattle: The University of Washington Press, 12-44.

Laforest, M. 1994. 'L'art d'écouter une histoire'. In: J. Bres (ed.), *Le récit oral suivi de Questions de narrativité*. Montpellier, Praxiling, 103-112.

Laforest, M. 1996. 'De la manière d'écouter les histoires: la part du narrataire'. In: M. Laforest (ed.), *Autour de la narration*. Québec, Nuit blanche éditeur, 73-96.

Laforest, M. 2001. 'Dire et redire: la constellation narrative'. *Revue Québécoise de Linguistique*, 29(1), 155-178.

Norrby, C. 1995. 'Vad är en berättelse – egentligen?'. In A-M. Ivars, A-M. Londen, L.

Nyholm, M. Saari & M. Tandefelt (eds.), *Svenskans beskrivning* (no. 21), Lund: Lund University Press, 208-217.

EVA WESTIN

Norrby, C. 1997. 'Berättelseannonsering i vardagssamtal'. In G. Håkansson, L. Lötmarker, L. Santesson, J. Svensson & Å. Viberg (eds.), *Svenskans beskrivning* (no. 22), Lund: Lund University Press, 82-96.

Norrick, N.R. 1998a. 'Retelling Stories in Spontaneous Conversation'. *Discourse processes*, 25(1), 75-97.

Norrick, N.R. 1998b. 'Retelling Again'. *Narrative Inquiry*, 8(2), 373-378.

Norrick, N.R. 2000. *Conversational Narrative. Storytelling in Everyday Talk.* Amsterdam/Philadelphia: John Benjamins.

Revaz, F. 1995. *Frontières du récit* (Thèse de doctorat). Université de Lausanne.

van Dijk, T.A. 1980. 'Story comprehension: an introduction'. *Poetics*, 9, 1-21.

Westin, E. 2003. *Le récit conversationnel en situation exolingue de français – formes, types et functions* (Doctoral thesis) (Études Romanes no. 68). Lund: Lund University Press.

The Awareness of Context in Second Language Acquisition Theories

Karen Lund

Abstract

The aim of the article is to review how some of the dominant SLA theories conceive of the learner and to what extent contextual factors are integrated in the theory building. I take a point of departure in Norton's interesting studies on migrants in Canada. My assumption is that second language acquisition takes place in and through interaction with target language speakers or writers, influenced by the socio-cultural conditions of historical time and space. To further the theoretical discussions, I present an approach to language that is different from the linguistic approach which dominates SLA theories, and I present an ecological approach to second language acquisition and pedagogy which may constitute a promising perspective to second language acquisition theory construction.

1. INTRODUCTION

The aim of the article is to compare dominant Second Language Acquisition (SLA) theories with socio-cultural perspectives on the learning of a second language in order to get a better understanding of how SLA theories conceive of the learner, and to see if and how contextual factors are integrated in the analyses of SLA processes.

I build on the assumption that learning a second language takes place through interaction and participation with native and non-native speakers of the target language, and that the social and cultural conditions that the learners meet, are influential for their possibilities to acquire the new language. Language acquisition does not take place in a speechless vacuum, and the learner cannot develop new language faculties without possibilities to interact in the target language. The language learner is a social actor, and language learning is a social practice which takes place in as well as through social interaction and participation in the communities (e.g. Vygotsky 1978, 1986, Wenger 1998) With this point of departure, contextual conditions, as well as possibilities and barriers for participation, become important issues in a theory on Second Language Acquisition in order to generate new theoretical insights.

As part of a larger project on integration and language learning[1] my reference point is, among others, the integration of migrants and refugees in the Danish society.

I am influenced and inspired among others by Vygotsky's theories (e.g.1978, 1986) and his emphasis on locating the individual within collective, material and historical conditions, which further entails a foregrounding of not only individuality but also sociality, and a focus on language as socially constructed. In this article I specifically take a point of departure in Bonny Norton's interesting work on migrants in Canada (e.g. 2000). The questions Norton wants to answer represent a relatively new and interesting set of perspectives on language learning processes. Questions like: What opportunities are available to second language speakers? What happens when target language speakers avoid interaction with second language speakers? When will a language learner take risks, and why? (Norton 2000:16). My question in this article is: Can existing SLA theories contribute with adequate answers to such questions?

2.   A SOCIOLOGICAL MODEL

As an analytical framework to mirror the SLA theories I use Layder's so-called resource map for research which has theory generation as a primary aim. In the model he seeks to incorporate macro- and micro-sociological features (Layder 1993 in Norton 2000). The model contains four research elements: *Context, setting, situated activity* and *individual actors*. The four elements are interconnected and each of them has a particular research focus.

Layder identifies *context* as the element which implicates:
  – The macro social organization
  – Values, traditions
  – Forms of social and economic organization
  – Power relations within the social formation (defined as legally sanctioned forms of ownership, control and distribution)

In connection with ethnic minorities' integration, context is reflected in issues concerning organized and institutionalized learning, settlement, the constraints of economy, language and integration policy – all features which are not peripheral to language learning, but central to its effectiveness, its success, and to its design. (Candlin in Norton 2000: xvi).

Setting focuses on the intermediate social organization in its already established social and institutional structure:

- Work-related institutions (state, bureaucracies, labour markets, hospitals, social work agencies, penal and mental institutions).
- Non-work-related institutions (leisure activities, sports and social clubs).

Setting is the already established social and institutional structure and practices within which the situated activities occur. The organization of the setting and the practices plays a predominant role in a language learner's possibilities and barriers for participation and interaction. Choices are already made before the learner enters a given institution.

Situated activity focuses on the face-to-face or mediated social activity:

- With focus on emergent meanings, understandings and definitions of the situation, as these affect and are affected by contexts and settings, and the subjective dispositions of individuals.

The situated encounters are significant for language learners without which the language learning process cannot proceed as the social interactive activities have direct implications for success and failure in language learning.

The individual actor is defined both as an individual and a collective self with multiple identities:

- Individuals identified both as selves and as social persons.
- Individual and collective identity.
- Struggle between the individuality and collectivity of the self.
- Emphasis on the dynamism and the variability inherent in the individual's motivation.

– Motivation defined as a struggle between the individual investment of capital and the constraining effects of macro elements
of context and setting.

Social actors do not act independently of social structures and they do
not exist outside of social practice. Individuals are context dependant
persons whose social roles within their social networks crucially affect
their opportunities for language learning, and their willingness to take
up those that become available. The social circumstances thus condition
the learner's relative success and failure.

Social activity, setting, and context all directly influence the experiences and possibilities of the individual actor.

As Duranti puts it: People in interaction – in acts of communication
– are people engaged in coordinated behaviours which not only imply
but also produce worldviews, including local notions of person or self
(Geertz 1973). To be standing in a line to get into the theatre not only
implies a set of assumptions and knowledge on how to get access to a
seat for a public performance, it also communicates notions of public
order, individual rights, and social cooperation. To refuse to be in line
is also a communicative act which publicly asserts defiance of public
norms and criticism of the rights and duties implied by those norms.
(Duranti 1997: 37).

With the model I want to reflect the interaction of the different
layers but also how they are incorporated and part of each other.

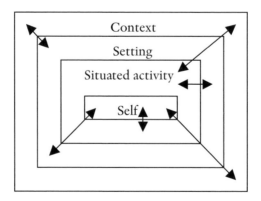

Fig. 1: A multi-layered model

KAREN LUND

With the objective of making a critical review through influential second language acquisition theories in order to see how socio-cultural dimensions are considered as an integral and influential player in the acquisition process, I will see which influence the different layers of the model are granted in SLA theories. Does the interplay between them and among them play an active role in theoretical frameworks of SLA? To what extent is a socio-cultural perspective integrated in SLA-theories?

3. A LANGUAGE MODEL

As another reflective means with focus on the linguistic domain I shall shortly present my conception of the relationship between language and context. I find it important to emphasize the dynamic interplay between and among grammatical, semantic and pragmatic functions and their interrelated contributions to the linguistic expression, utterance or text. The semantic and pragmatic functions respectively get their meaning potentials by means of an active interplay between the different linguistic and non-linguistic conditions of the context.

Common to all languages, grammatical functions are in most cases combined with semantic and pragmatic functions which facilitate the learning process. Examples in Danish where the semantic potentials are weak or absent are gender, number and definiteness on adjectives and inversion in declaratives.

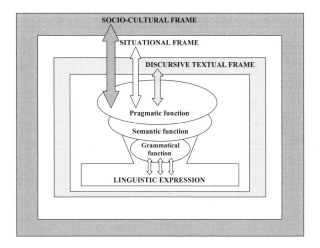

Fig. 2: A functional language model. (Lund 1997: 312)

The model in Fig. 2 describes the interrelatedness between a linguistic expression, its grammatical, semantic and pragmatic functions and the contextual linguistic factors such as linguistic context and discourse and the linguistic and non-linguistic situational and socio-cultural factors at micro and macro levels.

The model can be read in the following way: A linguistic expression/ utterance is decoded by the listener or reader by means of grammatical, semantic and pragmatic knowledge. The semantic and pragmatic functions, however, are only understood when related to the linguistic and non-linguistic context in a dynamic interplay between and among these different layers. In the interpretation process the interlocutor relies on the multilayered linguistic and non-linguistic cues embodied in the linguistic expression. The combination or interrelatedness of the grammatical, semantic and pragmatic function is mapped by the graphic intersections between the three functions.

Based on Lund (1997) my assumption is that second language acquisition takes place through the form-meaning mapping and the embodiment of meaning in the coding and decoding of linguistic expressions, utterances or texts. The process of production, understanding and interaction rely on a multitude of linguistic and communicative cues internalized in the development of the language, and to make communication possible and relatively fluent coding and decoding rely on a multitude of internalized routinized language (Pawley and Syder 1983, Lund 1997: 125ff). In section 9 I will elaborate my approach to language.

4. SECOND LANGUAGE ACQUISITION THEORIES FROM A CRITICAL LEARNING PERSPECTIVE

4.1 SLA THEORIES WITH FOCUS ON INNATENESS AND NATURAL LEARNING PROCESSES

Dominant SLA theories represented by, among others, Chomsky's theories of *Universal Grammar* and Krashen's *natural input hypotheses*, rely on an inborn Universal Grammar or a Language Acquisition Device (LAD) which only needs minimal triggering from the environment to make language acquisition happen. Contextual factors are disregarded as having little influence on the development, and the learning process is considered to take place independently of micro and macro contextual conditions.

According to the theories of *natural sequences* of SLA, all learners pass through the same developmental sequences in the acquisition of certain morphemes and certain syntactic structures. The acquisition takes place independently of background variables such as age, educational background and mother tongue. There may be differences as to how fast learners pass through the structural sequences, and some learners may add a stage or two. But none of the stages are left out. The universality of the sequences relies on a genetically based hypothesis of a LAD, and the learner can be described as a mere spectator of evolving grammatical structures (Lund 1996, 1997).

Pienemann's *processability theory* deals with the development or emergence of a learner grammar, and spells out the processing prerequisites that are posited as necessary for the acquisition of grammatical rules at different developmental stages. He thereby establishes an acquisitional hierarchy based on processing prerequisites. (Pienemann 1998, Glahn et al. 2001).

These approaches all focus on the development of grammatical structure, and they all disregard a possible influence from semantic and pragmatic functions. The research focus is on language learning as a natural, genetically based implicit process. Neither linguistic conditions such as semantics nor pragmatic use of language are considered to influence natural developmental sequences. Nor are social conditions such as social situational acts, setting and macro context taken into consideration.

From a methodological point of view this approach implies serious inadequacy: If functional or social issues are disregarded in the methodological framework, they will evidently never show up as implicative factors of SLA. A structural approach will not reveal whether or not the learning process is highly influenced by the relationship between form and function, as semantic and pragmatic functions are not considered in the theoretical framework. (Lund 1996, 1997). Neither will it get us closer to an understanding of the impact of contextual factors and social interaction.

A good example of the difference between theories excluding or including contextual issues as implicative for SLA we find in Krashen's *i+1 hypothesis* compared to Vygotsky's *Zone of Proximal Development* (ZPD). As stated by Thorne (2000: 226) the two metaphors have unconvincingly been equated:

According to the i+1 hypothesis 'We acquire by understanding language that contains structure a bit beyond our current level of comprehension (i+1)' and 'When communication is successful, when the input is understood, and when there is enough of it, i+1 will be provided automatically' (Krashen 1982: 21-22, Lund 1997: 79). According to Krashen, access to input containing x+1 will always be there if the learner is exposed to 'natural' input.

Vygotsky's ZPD, by sharp contrast, involves what an individual can accomplish or perform in collaboration with for example a more competent speaker. Hence i+1 is a metaphor about language input quality and its effect on language acquisition, and Vygotsky's ZPD is a theoretical approach to emergence and development of language based on the close analysis of activity made possible through collaboration. Krashen's i+1 and Vygotsky's ZPD are unrelated in various aspects:

- Their conceptualization: a passive body exposed to input versus collaborative activity.
- Their philosophical underpinnings: the learner as autonomous versus personal ability co-constructed through activity with other people and artefacts in the environment.
- Focus of the learning process: 'natural' implicit learning analogous to the child's first language acquisition versus active learning through collaboration.

(Thorne 2000: 226-227)

4.2 SLA THEORIES WITH FOCUS ON INDIVIDUAL DIFFERENCES
A great deal of mainstream SLA literature is concerned with individual differences and their implications for the language learning process. Learners are for example categorized as:

- introverted – extroverted
- inhibited – uninhibited
- risk avoiders – risk takers
- inflexible – flexible

The learner is described as being equipped with these characteristics and contextual factors are not included in the analyses and hence not regarded to play any role for the learning process. What we find in the theory are static non-dynamic approaches to the individual, where socio-cultural conditions are not considered to have any influence on a learner's risk avoiding or risk taking uniform identity. Possibilities granted by social conditions are not discussed as having any bearing on the identity of the learner.

The approach represents an essentialist view on the learner as equipped with or without certain qualities, and the impact of social conditions and inequitable relations of power is disregarded.

The same essentialist approach to the language learner is foregrounded in research on the so-called good language learner (e.g. Rubin 1975):

'The good language learner'

- seeks out opportunities to learn the language
- is highly motivated
- has good attention to detail
- can tolerate ambiguity
- has low level of anxiety

The good language learner can choose and make contacts by means of specific inborn qualities. Whether attitudes of interlocutors may have an impact or even change 'the good language learner' is not taken into consideration.

4.3 MOTIVATION AND SLA

According to Gardner and Lambert's influential theories on motivation (1972) the language learner's access to the target language community depends on the learner's motivation. Learner attitude determines motivation which determines learning facilitation, and the level of anxiety determines the developmental profile of the learner.

Most favourable, according to Gardner and Lambert, is an integrative motivation where the learner wants to learn the language successfully in order to obtain a relationship as close as possible with the native community and within a wide range of functional contexts.

A similar approach to motivation is to be found in Krashen's *input theory* and his hypothesis of an affective filter. The hypothesis predicts that affective conditions such as lacking motivation, lack of self-esteem, stress and anxiety may cause a high affective filter and consequently prevent input from reaching the Language Acquisition Device and become intake. Positive motivation on the other hand may lower the filter and implicate favourable learning conditions.

As stated by Krashen:

> When the filter is 'down' and appropriate comprehensible input is presented (and comprehended), acquisition is inevitable. In fact unavoidable and cannot be prevented – the language 'mental organ' will function just as automatically as any other organ.
>
> (Krashen 1985: 4)

The problem with Krashen's affective filter is that it is never explained how and under what conditions the affective filter will be low or high. As stated by McLaughlin:

> The role of the affective filter in Krashen's theory appears to be that of *deus ex machina*, allowing for any and all results. But appeals to poorly defined mechanisms do little to further understanding.
>
> (McLaughlin 1987: 54)

The affective filter hypothesis is not adequately theorized and may be claimed to function as a sort of 'repair hypothesis' helping to explain the variability of the learning process (Lund 1997: 81, 245).

These SLA theorists do recognize that language learners do not live in idealized homogeneous communities. But the heterogeneity and the complexity are generally framed uncritically, and socio-cultural diversity is not considered influential to the learner's pre-existing favourable or disfavourable characteristics, or to a given motivational approach to the society and the native speakers. It is disregarded that a person's identity will change in accordance with changing social and economic relations.

The concept of motivation thus conceives of the language learner as having a unified static and coherent identity which organizes the type and the intensity of a language learner's motivation. Instrumental and integrative motivation presupposes a unitary, fixed and ahistorical language learner who desires to acquire the target language either for utilitarian purposes, such as work, or for successful integration. Socio-cultural diversity and power relations which might prevent or facilitate the learner's access to interaction with the native speakers are not discussed.

But as emphasized by Norton (2000: 10) motivation is far from unified and coherent. Motivation and affection cannot be understood apart from the learner's relationship to larger social structures that may affect and conflict with the desire to speak. Dependant of social relations and power relations the learner's motivational investment may be complex, contradictory and changing over time and space.

With the notion of *investment*, Norton wants to emphasize the dynamism and the variability inherent in motivation, and the struggle between the individual investment of symbolic capital and the facilitating or constraining effects of the macro elements of context and setting.

According to Candlin, motivational theory has until recently been largely innocent of any social engagement (Norton 2000: xviii). The focus on the individual self and the personal belief structures leads to a disregard of the influence of context and setting.

4.4 THE ACCULTURATION THEORY

Schumann's acculturation theory (1976, 1978, Lund 1997) differs from the theories mentioned till now in that it highlights the socio-cultural context without neglecting the individual and the group.

The acculturation hypothesis claims that the degree to which the learner acculturates to the target language group will control the degree to which he acquires the target language. If acculturation does not take place, instruction in the target language will be of limited benefit to the language learner. Most people working in the field of SLA education will probably agree on that. It is important to notice, however, that all foreign language instruction – defined as language instruction and learning taking place apart from the target language communities – is completely biased by this assumption.

Schumann's 'acculturation' concept is a cluster of two groups of variables – social factors and affective factors, and acculturation is the social and psychological integration of the individual with the target language group (Schumann 1978).

If a learner does not learn the target language, it is because he is insufficiently acculturated socially and psychologically. Thus, social and psychological distance between the learner and the target language community accounts for a learner's pidginized speech and vice versa.

Schumann's acculturation theory is expressed in the following three assumptions.

Assumption 1:

> If a second language group is inferior or subordinate to the target language group, it will resist learning the second language.

The second language group is categorized as inferior and subordinate – a static picture that does not take into account whether the minority group has developed into being inferior and subordinate by being treated as inferior to the majority. Neither is it considered whether some learners might continue to have aspirations to learn the second language even though they are marginalized. Another issue is the unitary, static view on the target language group implied in the assumption. The influence of changing target language groups, changing purposes and changing contexts is not taken into consideration.

In assumption 2 an assimilation strategy is claimed to maximize contact with target language groups and to enhance the learner's SLA, similar to Lambert and Gardner's theory on integrative motivation (1972).

Assumption 2:

> If members of the second language learning group give up their lifestyles and values and adopt those of the target language group, they will maximize their contact with the target language group and enhance SLA.

If the migrant is already marginalized, and if the target language users do not welcome the migrant's positive attitudes, it may be of little effect that he or she gives up his or her lifestyle and values. The question is what will happen if the target language group does not want to welcome the attempts of the migrant group to assimilate.

Assumption 3:

> Positive attitudes between the target language group and the second language group will enhance SLA.

If we define integration to be a relational process, we probably cannot disagree with this assumption. On the other hand, it assumes an idealistic power-free relationship, and the continuous changes of the 'when', 'where', and the 'who' are not discussed.

In the acculturation hypothesis differences are not theorized in terms of unequal relations of power, which compromise efforts by language learners to interact with target language speakers and promote SLA. Those who are marginalized are responsible, and assimilation is seen as the goal – acculturation is assimilation. The psychological load of an assimilation strategy is not taken into consideration.

A final theoretical problem is that the acculturation hypothesis cannot be falsified, as social and psychological distance is impossible to test (Lund 1997: 100, McLaughlin 1987). Furthermore, Schumann who also belongs to the theorists around the hypothesis of natural structural sequences does not explain in which way social and psychological conditions influence the interlanguage development. Why are certain linguistic areas affected and others not? The same question can be asked in relationship to Krashen's affective filter.[2]

5. 'NATURAL' LANGUAGE LEARNING

Spolsky (1989) has focus on the advantages of learning a second language in real-life contexts. He has four claims about the advantages of the 'natural' language learning context:

1. The 'natural' language learning context gives possibilities to use language for authentic communication and possibilities for negotiation of meaning.
2. The learner is surrounded by fluent language speakers.
3. The outside world is open and stimulating with a multitude of contextual clues for understanding language in use.
4. In natural learning, where attention is on meaning, the target language speaker makes an effort to see that language is comprehensible.

We cannot disagree with the ideas implied in these four claims. To what extent, however, do they describe real-life possibilities?

1. According to Norton's data, target language speakers are frequently unwilling to engage in negotiation of meaning with language learners. Besides it may be questionable whether language learners frequently engage in real-life negotiation of meaning. They are probably more likely to abstain from negotiations of meanings in order not to lose face

and self esteem. Rather, what many SLA learners learn is perhaps not to negotiate in order to hide their lack of understanding.

From an acquisitional point of view, one may also ask how much the learner profits from the kind of negotiation taking place under the time pressure of real life interaction, or whether negotiation of meaning most frequently is used just to overcome acute communicative problems. Maybe the classroom is a much better place for negotiation of meaning, and one from which educators could profit by organizing frequent occasions for such negotiations.

2. My question to this assumption is: Are migrants in fact surrounded by fluent language speakers? Perhaps: If they are married to target language speakers or if they work with them in a context where they are accepted as communication partners.

3. Concerning the third claim: Whether or not real life constitutes an open and stimulating world, depends on the social realities the learner meets. Reality for many migrants is that they have no access to interaction with native speakers. They have low status jobs at workplaces where they are not even regarded to be *peripheral legitimate participants.*[3]

In the next chapter I will look at some examples to see to what extent the world constitutes a 'nice welcoming place' for migrants.

6. EXAMPLES FROM REAL LIFE

The experience of the women in Bonny Norton's research programme tells us another story about integration compared to the theories I have presented till now. Based on her empirical study Norton (2000: 112ff) concludes that:

- Natural language learning does not necessarily offer language learners opportunities to learn in an open and stimulating environment in which learners are surrounded by fluent speakers of the target language, who generously ensure that the learner understands the communication, and who are prepared to negotiate meaning in an egalitarian and supportive atmosphere.
- Natural language learning is frequently marked by inequitable asymmetrical relations of power in which language learners strug-

gle for access to social networks that will give them opportunities to practice their English in safe and supportive environments.

– The outside world is frequently hostile and uninviting. Native speakers are often impatient with the language learners' attempts at communication and likely to avoid rather than negotiate meaning with them.

– Based on the multitude of contextual clues that the learners picked up, their impressions were that native speakers did not like to talk or work with migrants.

According to these findings the conclusion is that the learners have difficulty in being accepted as so-called *legitimate speakers* (Bourdieu 1997). They are deprived of *the right to speech* defined as the right of speakers not only to be understood, but also to be believed, obeyed, respected, distinguished. An asymmetrical relation between speakers and an unequal access to symbolic power relations prevents this. An important research question is how migrants get access to the so-called cultural capital, including linguistic capital.

Despite being good language learners and despite their strong drive to communicate, the women in Norton's study had difficulty speaking under conditions of marginalization, even though they did not have inhibited personalities and they were not unwilling to make mistakes. Often they felt marginalized because they felt positioned as immigrants and 'less worthy' than Canadians. In this way they were affected by the social relations of power in their daily interaction.

As experienced by these women, access to symbolic resources – such as language, education and friendship, and material resources such as capital goods, real estate and money – does not relate only to the macro level of powerful institutions, such as the legal system, the education system and social welfare system, but also to the micro level of everyday social encounters between people with differential access to symbolic and material resources – encounters which inevitably take place through language.

We have seen that the SLA theorist regards the condition for establishment of communication as already secured, whereas, in real situations, that is the essential question. The SLA theorist:

> takes for granted the crucial point, namely that people who talk to each
> other, are 'on speaking terms', that those who speak regard those who

listen as worthy to listen and that those who listen regard those who speak as worthy to speak.

(Bourdieu 1977: 648 in Norton 2000: 113)

7. THE CONCEPT OF IDENTITY

A question to be asked is if the concept of identity presented in the theories are adequate. Is it so that every person has an essential, unique, fixed and coherent core (introvert/extrovert; motivated/unmotivated) as claimed by the theories analysed?

Or rather, is it so that the individual is diverse, contradictory, dynamic and changing over historical time and social space, and that the individual has an identity with multiple changing identities?

Do we take an essentialist static point of departure, or do we consider SLA as a process taking place in social interaction in communities where the context plays an important role for learning to be facilitated and for learning to take place?

According to Norton (2000) identity construction must be understood with reference to relations of power between language learners and target language speakers, and accordingly as changing over time and space. Social identity is very important for the learner's possibilities. Is there somebody with whom to interact? Is the learner considered to be a legitimate speaker or is he excluded and stigmatized beforehand? How do such conditions influence the learner's self-esteem?

Marginalization has an impact on learners' motivation. The learners' identity will change in accordance with social and economic relations. Eventually even the highly motivated learners may learn the lesson if they are met with ambivalent attitudes over and again. They may enter the new world highly motivated with all intentions of integrating and learning the language as fast as possible. But if they are marginalized and afterwards blamed for their inability to acculturate, they will probably give up and come to the conclusion: What's the point? The result of a vicious circle.

From this perspective language learning is dependent not only on the individual learner's personal potentials. Personal potentials and the use of strategies are important for the individual in his effort to cope with the multitude of different possibilities and barriers. But the learner cannot – once and for all – be regarded as a good or inhibited language learner. The situations and the people the learner meets are decisive as to whether the learner uses his potentials or feels so marginalized that he gives up; what he learns may be how to cope with not even being considered a peripheral legitimate participant. He learns to keep silent, or he gets aggressive for not being accepted as a participant.

8. THE THEORIES AND THE IMPACT OF CONTEXTUAL FACTORS – A SUMMARY

What is common to the analyzed approaches to second language acquisition can be summed up as follows:

1. We have seen an artificial distinction between the individual and the social with no integration and interrelation between the language learner and the language learning context.

2. The theories disregard how relations of power and inequities in the social world impact on social interaction between second language learners and target language speakers.

3. The theories have not developed a comprehensive theory of identity that integrates the language learner and the language learning context. Identity is not identified as being negotiated through social action, setting and context.

9. LANGUAGE AS LINGUISTIC STRUCTURE OR SOCIO-CULTURAL PRACTICE?

A common feature is that most SLA research – from Behaviourism to Universal Grammar, over the theories of natural sequences of acquisition to processability theory – including the theories discussed in this article – are based on a structuralist conception of language. A structuralist language approach implies that the theoretical framework cannot account for context factors and their possible influence on SLA. Neither can a structuralist approach account for the influence of semantic and pragmatic factors on SLA (Lund 1997).

Structuralists conceive of language as signs having idealized meanings and of linguistic communities as being relatively homogeneous. Structuralism cannot account for the struggle over the social meanings that can be distributed to signs in a given language. Signs have idealized meanings – they are synchronic, universal, arbitrary sign relations.

Poststructuralists, on the other hand, take the position that practices of societies are sites of struggle, and that linguistic communities are heterogeneous areas characterized by conflicting claims to truth and power. A poststructuralist approach marks a shift from synchrony to diachrony and historicity, a widespread recognition of the fluidity of cultures, and an interest in multiculturalism and trans-national communities.

Bourdieu emphasizes the importance of language not as an autonomous system – as proposed by the structuralists – but as a system that is actively defined by socio-political processes, including bureaucratic institutions such as schools. For Bourdieu one cannot discuss a language without taking into consideration the social conditions that allow for its existence. A language itself is a set of practices that imply not only a particular system of words and grammatical rules, but also an often forgotten or hidden struggle over the symbolic power of a particular way of communicating, with particular systems of classification, address and reference forms, specialized lexicon, and metaphors (Bourdieu 1982: 31 in Duranti 1997: 45).

It is important not to forget that a certain linguistic expression can perform an action (e.g. a request, offer, and apology) only to the extent to which there is a system of dispositions, *a habitus*, already shared in the community (Bourdieu 1982: 133). Such systems are, in turn, reproduced by daily speech acts, organized and given meaning by institutions such as the school, the family, the work place, which are not only established to exclude others, but also to keep those who are in them under control, to make sure that the acts they perform and the meanings they attribute to such acts remain within an acceptable range (Pandolfi 1991 in Duranti 1996: 46).

These reflections are important because they link individual acts to larger frames of reference, including the notion of community. They are also important because they give an explanatory framework to intercultural communication and miscommunication.

Language is a powerful instrument. If you do not speak the target language, you do not have access to networks, to forming relationships, or to participate. Language is a social practice, and language mediates the interaction between human beings and the social world. It is a mistake, however, to presume that the responsibility for access to obtaining communicative competence lies individually with the learner, and that he or she can control his or her access to interaction with the native speakers.

The complexity of interaction cannot be reduced to grammar or reduced to longer or shorter rituals learnt by heart – which is necessary – but not enough. In any interaction something new will happen, and the big challenge is to be able to cope with all the new information. You cannot predict the topic and the running changes of topic. You are in a continuous negotiation on the right to take the floor, and consequently a risk is at stake as you hereby claim the right to be accepted as a legitimate speaker. As a not-fully-competent speaker you also run the continuous risk of losing face by exposing your lack of linguistic knowledge, your knowledge of how to interact or communicate, and your lack of content knowledge, etc.

To be a competent speaker means to be able to do things with a language as part of larger social activities which are culturally organized and must, therefore, be culturally interpreted. Speaking is a social activity involving more than linguistic expressions. Language is more than representations of the objects of the world, and words carry a power with them that goes beyond the description and identification of people, objects, properties, and events (Duranti 1997: 19f). Language is a tool through which our social and cultural world is constantly described, evaluated, and reproduced.

As Hymes wrote in his criticism of Chomsky's notion of competence, it is necessary

> ... to account for the fact that a normal child acquires knowledge, not only as grammatical, but also as appropriate. He or she acquires competence as to when to speak, when not, and as to what to talk about with whom, when, where, in what manner. In short, a child becomes able to accomplish a repertoire of speech acts, to take part in speech events, and to evaluate their accomplishment by others. This competence, moreover, is integral with attitudes, values, and motivations concerning language, its features and uses, and integral with competence for, and attitudes towards, the interrelation of language with the other code of communicative conduct.
>
> (Hymes 1972: 277-278)

Speaking is a continuous process of contextualization. According to Gumperz (1996), interactional work is performed through a vast range of contextualization cues – indexical signs which let people know how interaction is expected to proceed. Contextualization cues help speakers signal and hearers interpret what the activity is, how semantic content is to be understood, and how each utterance relates to what precedes or follows. These features are habitually used and perceived but rarely consciously noted and almost never talked about directly. Therefore they may function as hidden mechanisms of power and marginalization (Gumperz 1982: 131, Lund 2000).

Language, as Bakhtin reminds us, is always dialogical, about something, and reflecting other voices as well as our own. It is shaped by the context and at the same time it shapes the context (van Lier 2003: 158). It is not a transmission of 'packets' of information from one person to another in monological or dialogical speech events, but the result of co-constructing meaning, working together.

According to Bourdieu and other social theorists, we are dominated by unconscious dispositions inculcated through participation in routine interactions. Ritualized, formalized language coerces speakers and hearers into accepting status quo (Bloch 1975 in Duranti 1997: 292). Routines are often implicit and unconscious to the speaker and the hearer and as such they can be an instrument of power where both speaker and hearer follow a path that has been already decided.

Talk is not simply a medium for the representation of a language-independent reality but also a ubiquitous resource for reproducing social reality, and hence existing relations of power and dependence (Duranti 1997: 11). Stereotypes are often routinely reproduced through the unreflective use of linguistic expressions that presuppose gender, race or class-differentiation. Languages may provide ready-made categorizations and generalizations that are accepted and taken for granted. Thus, linguistic practices may be important ways in which a homogeneous view of culture is reproduced.

9.2 CULTURE AND LANGUAGE

Language and culture are closely connected, and cultural conventions are expressed through language, and the way you communicate is influenced and shaped by the culture in which you live and work. Accordingly, language influences and is influenced by social conditions at multiple levels.

Culture as created through participation and practices is based on the assumption that any action, including verbal communication, has an inherently social, collective, and participatory quality. To speak a language means to be able to participate in interaction with a world that is always larger than us as individual speakers and even larger than what we can see and touch in any given situation. Words carry with them a myriad of possibilities for connecting us to other human beings, other situations, events, acts, beliefs, feelings.

This is due to the ability that language has to describe the world as well as its ability to connect us with its inhabitants, objects, places, and periods; each time reaffirming a socio-historical dimension of human action among others. It is through language that we, to a large extent, are members of a community of ideas and practices (Duranti 1997: 46).

10. NEW APPROACHES TO SECOND LANGUAGE ACQUISITION

10.1 SLA AND THEORY BUILDING

SLA is a process which takes place in interactions and through interactions – collectively and among individuals where individuals are defined both as selves and as social persons. SLA theory must therefore take off from a multifaceted approach including a socio-cultural as well as a cognitive perspective on learning. Learning takes place in interaction, practice and participation – covering the social dimension – and learning takes place through interaction, practice and participation – dealing with a cognitive dimension. As Rampton states: 'At present SLA could probably benefit from an enhanced sense of the empirical world's complex socio-cultural diversity', (Rampton 1995: 244).

Sociocultural approaches to learning, based on the central notions of mediation, historical and contextual situatedness, and human action have gained some currency in SLA theories but often as an add-on to former theories (Thorne 2000: 226) like the theories reviewed in this article. But as stated by Bourdieu, the transgression of disciplinary boundaries is a prerequisite for scientific advance.

10.2 AN ECOLOGICAL APPROACH TO SECOND LANGUAGE ACQUISITION

According to van Lier (2000) among others, an ecological approach suggests new ways of doing research in SLA. Ecology is the study of the relationship between all the various organisms and their physical environment. It is a complex, dynamic and messy field of study, which changes over time and space, about a complex and messy reality. Its primary requirement is, by definition, that the context is central, it cannot be reduced, and it cannot be pushed aside or into the background (Van Lier 2003: 144).

As second language learning is a process involving intra- as well as inter-psychological activity and occurs within micro and macro social contexts, this must be taken into account in the production of ecological robust research. Van Lier proposes a non-reductionist ecological approach to SLA, and probably in order not to be reductionist, he gives a broad definition of language as: The totality of linguistic activities and relationships among speakers and between speakers and the physical, social, personal, cultural, and historical world they live in (2000: 259).

His arguments for an ecological approach are based on a critique of three premises underlying standard scientific thinking which are also constitutive of the SLA theories analyzed in this article (2000: 246ff). The first premise is:

- It is necessary to simplify and select from the infinite variety of the real world.
- The simplest explanation that minimally accounts for the data is to be preferred – in accordance with Occam's razor.
- Problems must be broken down into their component elements and these must be analyzed one by one.

An ecological approach, on the contrary, shifts the emphasis on scientific reductionism to the notion of emergence. Instead of expecting that every phenomenon can be explained in terms of simpler phenomena or components, it says that at every level of development, properties emerge that cannot be reduced to those of prior levels.

The second premise is that learning takes place in the brain, by means of computational mechanisms that process information received by the senses. Whether the perspective is constructionist, behaviourist, or nativist, the underlying view of learning is that information is received and subsequently processed in the brain and incorporated into mental structures providing knowledge and skills of various kinds.

Ecology, on the contrary, says that not all of cognition and learning can be explained in terms of processes that go on inside the head. From an ecological perspective the learner is immersed in an environment full of potential meanings. These meanings become available gradually as the learner acts and interacts within this environment.

The third premise is that activity and interaction, or in general the context in which learning takes place, relates to learning in an indirect way, by feeding into the cognitive processes in the individual. An ecological approach asserts that the perceptual and social activity of the learner, and particularly the verbal and nonverbal interaction in which the learner engages, are central to an understanding of learning, and do not just facilitate learning.

However, this does not mean that learners are merely 'empty heads', as van Lier puts it. Rather, it means that cognition and learning rely on both representational (schematic, historical, cultural etc.) processes and systems and ecological (perceptual, emergent, action-based) processes and systems. Therefore language itself is both representational and ecological also, and its definition, its structure, and its use are inherently dialogical, as claimed by Bakhtin (1981).

An ecological approach to language learning avoids a narrow interpretation of language as words that are transmitted through the air, on paper, or along wires from a sender to a receiver. It also avoids seeing learning as something that happens exclusively inside a person's head. Ecological educators see language and learning as relationships among learners and between learners and the environment. This does not deny cognitive processes, but it connects those cognitive processes with social processes. Language is also connected with kinetic, prosodic, and other visual and auditory sources of meaning. The ecological perspective thus places a strong emphasis on contextualizing language into other semiotic systems and into the contextual world as a whole (Van Lier 2000: 258-59).

10.3 AFFORDANCE

In terms of learning, language emerges out of semiotic activity. The context is not just there to provide input to a passive recipient. The environment provides a so-called 'semiotic budget' within which the active learner engages in meaning-making activities together with others. The semiotic budget does not refer to the amount of input available, but to the opportunities for meaningful action that the situation affords (Van Lier 2000: 252).

To van Lier *affordance* (Gibson 1979) is a key-concept in an ecological approach to SLA. Affordances consist in the opportunities for interaction offered by all kinds of things in the environment. In terms of language learning, the environment is full of language that provides opportunities for learning to the active, participating learner. The linguistic world to which the learner has access, and in which (s)he becomes actively engaged, is 'full of demands, and requirements, opportunities and limitations, rejections and invitations, enablement and constraints – in short, affordances' (Shotter and Newton 1982: 34 in van Lier 2000: 253). An actively engaged participant is offered a myriad of opportunities for meaningful action and interaction – these opportunities are called affordances (Van Lier 2003).

It goes without saying that an ecological approach to SLA research is a complex and complicated affair. But the question is whether the results we reach – if we exclude complexities – will have any theoretical weight or implications for a deeper understanding of language learning and integration.

11. PEDAGOGICAL PERSPECTIVES

An ecological approach to the study of language has focus on the study of relationships – and to study what language does to a person and for a person in the multiplicity of semiotic ecosystems in which language operates and co-operates with other meaning-making processes (van Lier 2003: 145).

A holistic approach to second language acquisition where language learning is regarded to take place through social participation and practice, calls for new pedagogical approaches which create close links between what goes on in the classroom and activities outside the classroom – in everyday life, at work, and in education.

It is important that the pedagogical approach integrates a continuous interplay between the learning sites and the different sites outside the school – bringing life into school and school out in real life activities. You cannot dress people up to cope with real-life activities in classrooms isolated from the activities outside the classroom.

A way to create an active interaction between classroom activities and real-life activities can be established by means of ethnographic based learning possibilities where the learners study, solve problems, make projects, collaborate with each other and interact with people in real life situations as part of school work. (Risager 1994, Lund & Svendsen Pedersen 2003).

Learning the new language is of crucial importance for a second language learner, and very much so in a language homogeneous country like Denmark. But it is not enough to be communicatively competent. Success depends on access to interaction and use of the target language, and success depends both on the investment of the learner and the social conditions outside the classroom – in short on affordance. If you do not have strategies for coping with the problem of being accepted as a legitimate participant and a legitimate speaker, all the language in the world will not help you.

Therefore it is important to develop strategies for the creation of possible rooms of participation for individuals, to enable them to be accepted as legitimate participants and thus avoid being excluded. These issues of empowerment should be subject matter in teaching and learning.

Key words in modern language education – implicated by an ecological approach to language learning are: Activity based learning, collaborative learning, experiential learning, problem solving activities, and ethnographic approaches. Educational approaches based on these concepts satisfy the learning requirements of *the social self* as well as those of *the individual self*. When learning takes place through participation and practice and through explorations in the socio-cultural environment, the active learner is afforded with multiple possibilities for meaningful action and interaction, and with possibilities to study the world and to acquire the language while participating. When learning takes place collectively through explorative, experiential based activities, the learners are granted possibilities to acquire knowledge and understanding and to become communicatively competent language users through joint activities and problem-solving. The learners thus have opportunity to cognitively solve problems about the world and the language via inductive, deductive and analogical problem-solving processes in collaboration with other individuals.

For the development of strategic knowledge, learners must be aware of the possibilities – what are the affordances and how do migrants use the possibilities. It is part of the pedagogical responsibilities of teachers and schools to focus on opening the class and give the learners possibilities to discover, develop, and create strategies which facilitates access to the affordances and potential interlocutors of the target language communities. To be willing to take risks and grasp the opportunities that present themselves are both necessary conditions.

12. CONCLUSION

Context, settings, social institutions, interlocutors – factors at micro and macro level – play decisive roles for learning to take place. What is missing in many SLA theories is a multifaceted perspective on learning. Much has happened in SLA theories within the last two or three decades. SLA research has become a theoretical research area in its own right. But we must not be blindfolded in a specific approach to SLA. If we do not continue to reflect on the theoretical assumptions, the history of SLA theories as a research area in its own right may be very short.

If SLA takes place in – and through – interaction, we cannot deal with theories that disregard the influence of socio-cultural and socio-economic contexts at micro and macro level, unless of course we believe in an autonomous mental organ. But even then, all theorists agree that there is much more to language than linguistic structure.

So if we want to account for the acquisition of language understood as multilayered and influenced by micro and macro contextual factors, it has implications for theory building. If SLA takes place through participation and social practice, contextual factors at micro and macro level must be an integrated part of the theoretical framework of SLA. If we want to throw light on the influence of semantic and pragmatic function in SLA, the research methodology has to be based on a functional approach. And, if we hypothesize contextual factors to be crucial to the learning process we cannot disregard context in the research methodology.

A theoretical platform of SLA must necessarily raise questions like: What opportunities are available to second language learners to interact with target language speakers? What happens when target language speakers avoid interaction with second language speakers? Under what conditions are language learners introverted, sensitive to rejection, inhibited? When will language learners take risks, and why? If language use is a prerequisite for acquiring a new language, we must consider the language learner's possibilities of participating.

If the language learner's self-esteem is dependent on the way (s)he is looked upon, and if his or her access to being regarded as a legitimate speaker is important for his or her language acquisition process, we must analyse the contextual environment. In our analysis we must focus on the possibilities and barriers meeting the language learner in his or her effort to get in touch with the native speakers, and it becomes important to find out what are the social arrangements in a community that constrain or facilitate movement towards fuller participation. SLA theories must search, therefore, for linguistic and non-linguistic factors that facilitate or constrain the individual's or the group's access to participation.

13. EPILOQUE: THE DANGER OF CATEGORIES, OR HOW CATEGORIES NATURALIZE SLA THEORIES

Through the writing of this article it has become clear to me how categories can take possession of our conception of theories and hence of our understanding of the learner and what learning is about. Common to the theories I have discussed is that learners are categorized or put into categories as being introverted/extroverted, inflexible/flexible, etc. The good language learner is motivated, has a low level of anxiety, etc. The affective filter is there to cope with feelings. Acculturation takes place according to how groups are categorized. Motivation is something you have or do not have. And lots of things in SLA theories are claimed to be 'natural'.

How does the learner get stuck in a certain category? The process takes place like this: What we *do* is put into language and described as *action* – language itself being action and interaction – and when actions are generalized, and generalizations of the actions are categorized, categorizations change into categories. From here the risk of 'naturalization' of the categories seems to be impeding. Qua categorizations and the proceeding establishment of categories, the learner and the learning process becomes naturalized, hence natural and universal. Learners *are* inhibited or uninhibited; they do not *act* inhibited or uninhibited according to changing contextual conditions.

The risk is perhaps not so much that we transform socially constructed action into categories – which is necessary in order to analyze what is going on – but that we elevate categories to an existence in their own right, and that categories from here are naturalized and elevated into 'forever lasting' universals. Relationships are transformed into systems of categories. Categories freeze actions into static entities. Categories are elevated into theories and hence taken for granted – perhaps.

The construction of NPs (noun phrases) and VPs (verb phrases) is one of the best examples to show how we may be lured to see the world as static: We *categorize* and *categorizations* become *categories*. We

generalize and *universalize*; after that *generalizations* and *universalizations**
(which until this point did not exist as a NP) become *general* and *universal*, and what we *theorize* become *theories*. We follow a process where
NPs and complements seize the VPs and thus produce a transformation
whereby verbal actions become static categories.

From being relational and process-making, the concepts are transformed into static categories which we internalize and 'forever after'
take to be natural. We internalize these systems as part of our life-long
socialization – they become natural – are naturalized. We may not recognize them as governing our actions, our doings – our linguistic doings
or recognize the ideologies that we hereby produce and reproduce.

Individuals, however, are not equipped with specific coherent and
uniform identities. Individuals can enact multiple identities dependent
on socio-cultural contextual issues. Individuals are not what they *are*
but what they *do*. Motivation is not static but relational. And, like all
other concepts, power is not static and something 'out there'. Power
is a relation, and power relations are constantly renegotiated – though
sometimes under very difficult circumstances.

When categorized, and hence naturalized and universalized, motivation, feelings, personality, etc. lose their dynamic and variable potentials.
Individuals are locked up in universal, natural categories – positively
or negatively stigmatized.

If we are not willing to negotiate the categories and our hypothesized
universals, we may be trapped in a world of static categories and systems.
It is important always to keep in mind that theories on for example
second languages acquisition are nothing but theoretical possibilities
created by human beings, and they are there to be challenged by new
approaches to further understanding.

NOTES

1 The project 'Learning and Integration – Adults and Danish as a Second
   Language' is supported by The Danish National Research Council for the
   Humanities.
2 See Lund 1997 for a critical review of SLA theories and their methodologies.
3 The notion is introduced by Lave and Wenger (1991), and a legitimate
   peripheral participant is defined as a newcomer at a workplace who through
   interaction with colleagues, gradually becomes more and more experienced
   in the practises of a given community and eventually becomes a full member.

KAREN LUND

BIBLIOGRAPHY

Bakhtin, M. 1981. *The Dialogic Imagination. Four Essays by M. Bakhtin.* M. Holquist (ed.) and E. Emerson (translator). Austin, TX: University of Texas Press.

Bloch, M. 1975. Introduction. In: M. Bloch (ed.), *Political Language and Oratory in Traditional Society.* London: Academic Press, 1-28.

Bourdieu, P. 1977. 'The economics of linguistic exchange'. *Social Science Information,* 16 (6), 645-68.

Bourdieu, P. 1982. *Ce que parler veut dire.* Paris: Fayard.

Duranti, A. 1997. *Linguistic Anthropology.* Cambridge University Press.

Gardner, R.C. and Lambert, W.E. 1972. *Attitudes and Motivation in Second Language Learning.* Rowley, MA: Newbury House.

Gertz, C. 1973. *The Interpretation of Cultures.* New York: Basic Books.

Gibson, J.J. 1979. *The Ecological Approach to Visual Perception.* Boston, MA: Houghton Mifflin.

Glahn, E., G. Håkansson, B. Hammarberg, A. Holmen, A. Hvenekilde and K. Lund 2001. 'Processability in Scandinavian Second Language Acquisition'. *Studies in Second Language Acquisition* 23, 389-416.

Gumperz, J.J. 1982. *Discourse Strategies.* Cambridge University Press.

Gumperz, J.J. 1996. 'The Linguistic and Cultural Relativity of Conversational Inferences'. In: J.J. Gumperz and S.C. Levinson (eds.), *Rethinking Linguistic Relativity.* Cambridge University Press, 374-407.

Hutchins, E. 1995. *Cognition in the Wild.* Cambridge, MA: MIT Press.

Hymes, D. 1972. 'On Communicative Competence'. In: J.B. Pride and J. Holmes (eds.), *Sociolinguistics.* Harmondsworth: Penguin, 269-85.

Hymes, D. 1979. 'On communicative competence'. In C.J. Brumfit and K. Johnson (eds.), *The Communicative Approach to Language Teaching.* Oxford: Oxford University Press, 5-26.

Krashen, S.D.1982. *Principles and Practice in Second Language Acquisition.* Oxford: Pergamon.

Krashen, S.D. 1985. *The Input Hypothesis.* London/New York: Longman.

Lave, J. 1988. *Cognition in Practice.* Cambridge University Press.

Lave, J. and E. Wenger 1991. *Situated Learning: Legitimate Peripheral Participation.* Cambridge University Press.

Layder, D. 1993. *New Strategies in Social Research.* Cambridge. Polity Press.

Lund, K. 1996. 'Communicative Function and Language-Specific Structure in Second Language Acquisition: A Discussion of Natural Sequences of Acquisition'. In: E. Engberg-Pedersen et al., *Content, Expression and Structure in Danish Functional Grammar.* Amsterdam: John Benjamins, 385-420.

Lund, K. 1997. *Lærer alle dansk på samme måde. En længdeundersøgelse af voksnes tilegnelse af dansk som andetsprog.* Special-pædagogisk forlag.

Lund, K. 2000. 'Interkulturel kommunikation – at navigere i misforståelser'. *Modersmål-Selskabet,* 35-43.

Lund, K. & M. Svendsen Pedersen 2003. 'Dansk som andetsprog på Arbejde'. In: G.Ø. Nielsen, M.S. Pedersen and K. Lund, *Individuelle Læringsplaner og Kollektive Læringsrum – en Vejledning.* Integrationsministeriet, 6-41.

McLaughlin, B. 1987. *Theories of Second Language Learning.* London: Edward Arnold.

Norton, B. 2000. *Identity and Language Learning. Gender, Ethnicity and Educational Change.* London/New York: Longman.

Pawley, A. and F. Hodgett Syder 1983. 'Two Puzzzels for Linguistic Theory: Nativelike Selection and Nativelike Fluency. In: J.C. Richards and R.W. Schmidt (eds.), *Language and Communication*. Longman, 191-226.

Pienemann, M. 1998. *Language Processing and Second Language Development: Processability Theory*. Amsterdam: Benjamins.

Rampton, B. 1995. *Crossing: Language and Ethnicity Among Adolecents*. London: Longman.

Risager, K. 1994. 'Eleven som Etnograf'. *Sprogforum* 4, 49-54.

Rubin, J. 1975. 'What the 'good language learner' can teach us. *TESOL Quarterly*, 9, 41-51.

Schumann, J. 1976. 'Second Language Acquisition Research: Getting a More Global Look at the Learner'. *Language Learning* 26(2), 391-408.

Schumann, J. 1978. 'The acculturation model for second-language acquisition'. In: R.C. Gringras (ed.), *Second Language Acquisition and Foreign Language Teaching*. Washington, DC: Center for Applied Linguistics.

Shotter J. and J. Newton 1982. 'An ecological Approach to Cognitive Development: Implicate Orders, Joint Action and Intentionality'. In: G. Butterworth and P. Light (eds.), *Social Cognition: Studies of the Development of Understanding*. Chicago IL: University of Chicago Press.

Spolsky, B. 1989. *Conditions for Second Language Learning*. Oxford: Oxford University Press.

Thorne, S.L. 2000. 'Second language acquisition theory and the truth(s) about relativity'. In: J.P. Lantolf (ed.), *Sociocultural Theory and Second Language Learning*. Oxford: Oxford University Press, 219-243.

van Lier, L. 2000. 'From Input to Affordance: Social-Interactive Learning from an Ecological Perspective' In: J.P. Lantolf (ed.), *Sociocultural Theory and Second Language Learning*. Oxford University Press, 245-259.

van Lier, L. 2003. 'An Ecological-Semiotic Perspective on Language and Linguistics'. In: C. Kramsch (ed.) 2003, *Language Acquisition and Language Socialization: Ecological Perspectives*. London; Continuum, 140-163.

Vygotsky, L.S. 1978. *Mind in Society: The Development of Higher Psychological Processes*. Cambridge, MA: Harvard University Press.

Vygotsky, L.S. 1986. *Thought and Language*. Cambridge, MA: MIT Press.

Wenger, E. 1998: *Communities of Practice: Learning, Meaning, and Identity*. Cambridge: Cambridge University Press.

Wertsch, J. 1985. *Culture, Communication, and Cognition: A Vygotskian Perspective*. Cambridge, MA: Harvard University Press.

Authenticity and Textbook Dialogues

Hanne Leth Andersen

Abstract

A central goal of modern foreign language learning is mastery of the basic oral communication skills of listening and speaking, with specific focus on successful interaction between native and non-native speakers. This interaction in the target language is central to all curricula and instruction in modern languages, but current teaching methods are often based on explicit knowledge about linguistic structures on the sentence level and do not always provide a solid basis for the interpersonal level. In the paper I will show that the examples of dialogue in beginning French textbooks for Danish learners often provide material emphasizing sentence structure rather than the structure of dialogue. Knowledge about the grammar of dialogue is provided within research fields like politeness theory, conversation analysis and discourse analysis, but this knowledge does not seem to have been sufficiently integrated into modern language teaching, textbooks and frameworks for classroom interaction. Authentic dialogues in languages obey specific rules of politeness for interaction and are thus a good example of culture in language.

1. GOALS IN FOREIGN LANGUAGE TEACHING

Modern foreign language teaching distinguishes between several distinct goals, divided into specific competence requirements and knowledge at different levels. The *European Language Portfolio* provides a solid basis for this by identifying five different sets of competence requirements at six different levels (http://culture2.coe.int/portfolio/). The identification and detailed description of these competences in this document is an opportunity and a strong instrument for teachers to help learners see themselves as competent learners and language users at different phases of the acquisition route, instead of as imperfect students far from the native speaker competence that constitutes a much too remote and unreachable goal in foreign language teaching.

Indeed, a common and usually quite unreachable goal for both teachers and learners of foreign languages has often been the ideal of either written or oral native-like fluency, based on the assumption that knowledge about the language is the necessary means of attaining this ideal; the method and the vision of language learning is that solid or perfect knowledge *about* the language, more precisely about the language system, eventually generates, more or less automatically, solid or perfect performance in the language.

The idea of progression in foreign language teaching thus implies that the language system is built from the bottom up, from articles to nouns, adjectives and pronouns, verbs, negation and on to sentences. Foreign language teaching in many European countries, such as in France, primarily focuses on grammar and written language, and test only writing skills at the Baccalaureate exams. In France and Denmark, as well as in many other countries, the theories of language acquisition based on input and on comprehension have some influence on the prevalent ideas; however, if one looks at the structure and dialogues of the textbooks it becomes clear that there is still a firm belief in many teaching traditions that knowledge of grammar comes first.

It should be clear though that progression in foreign language learning does not involve a progression in explicit knowledge of grammar, but rather a progression in the learner's receptive and productive skills – in communication. In Denmark, the ongoing reforms of the primary, lower-secondary and secondary schools prioritize clear goals at each level, with communication at the first level, as research in acquisition emphasizes, and thus contain a clear idea about progression. This is well in line with the *European Language Portfolio*, which offers definitions of the five sets of skills: Two comprehension skills: listening and reading; two oral skills: oral interaction and oral language production, and one writing skill. All five sets of skills are divided into six levels, the *Basic User* (A1 and A2), the *Independent User* (B1 and B2), and the *Proficient User* (C1 and C2), and for each of these is a specific description of what the language user is able to perform.

As we can see below, the publication *Fremtidens sprogfag* ('Language teaching in the future'), issued by the Danish Ministry of Education in 2003, presents a progression in language learning that is very clearly not based on grammatical knowledge of morphology and syntax; instead it goes from the basic level of vocabulary training, including chunks and knowledge of scenarios to knowledge of the structure of conversation, use of chunks, text types, text parts and sentences, and then – only at

HANNE LETH ANDERSEN

the fourth level – to explicit knowledge of elementary morphology and syntax:

	Skills	Strategies	Linguistic knowledge	Content
5	Writing skills	Process-oriented writing	Language structure, morphology, syntax	All text types, literary and non-literary
4	Oral presentation	Oral presentation, knowledge of structure, subjects, vocabulary	Knowledge of elementary morphology and syntax	Society-related, culture-related and literary themes
3	Reading comprehension (understanding the written language)	Reading strategies (skimming, scanning, knowledge of text genre, vocabulary)	Knowledge of text structure, text type, paragraph, sentence	Well-known society- and culture-related themes
2	Conversational skills	Communication strategies	Knowledge of the structure of conversation, use of special terms and expressions (islands) and knowledge of scenarios	Close and accessible society- and culture-related themes
1	Listening comprehension (understanding the spoken language)	Listening strategies (guessing, understanding situations, vocabulary in situations)	Vocabulary training, linguistic islands, knowledge of scenarios	People-related themes

Fig. 1: Fremtidens sprogfag, 41.[1]

The vision is that of input first, followed by comprehension training, vocabulary training in well-known scenarios, dialogue training, and then grammar as a tool to be used once some elementary, core language skills have been established. The progression in this document constitutes an important basis for the descriptions of foreign language teaching in the upper-secondary school reform of 2005, which underlines the importance of input and communication, and of knowledge about culture in communication and, in addition, that oral and written communicative skills are the main focus in formal evaluations and exams. The new guidelines strongly emphasize that the ability to communicate well counts more than a low rate of error, maintaining the idea of progression in which explicit knowledge about grammar provides the best results at the highest levels.

In the Danish reform of the primary and lower secondary school (the 'grundskole') in 2003, the description of the common goals (*Fælles Mål*)[2] is quite similar; here the focus on oral skills is also very clear, although, as we shall see, the focus seems to be on oral skills in the interview genre.

2. COMMUNICATION AND CULTURE

Having underlined the importance of a clear definition of the partial goals and progression of language learning, I would like to stress another important point. Knowledge about culture is a fundamental communicative competence in foreign language learning. Big C culture, as Claire Kramsch puts it (this volume), which presents literature as still very important in modern language teaching, but which also argues that culture is part of the language and communication aspect of foreign language teaching, albeit perhaps more implicitly. In 'Common goals' for French in primary and lower secondary schools, the vision of communication seems at first to be the sole exchange of questions and answers, which is not an authentic informal means of communication in any culture, but then subsequently it mentions the use of basic French forms of politeness and also the use of idioms and culturally bound expressions.[3]

In the *European Language Portfolio*, spoken interaction at level A1 reveals a focus on questions and answers too, and A2 focuses on the exchange of information but also introduces short social exchanges, which might very well entail knowledge of culturally determined language use.

HANNE LETH ANDERSEN

	A1	A2
Spoken Interaction	I can interact in a simple way provided the other person is prepared to repeat or rephrase things at a slower rate of speech and help me formulate what I'm trying to say. *I can ask and answer simple questions in areas of immediate need or on very familiar topics.*	I can communicate in *simple and routine tasks* requiring a simple and direct exchange of information on familiar topics and activities. I can handle very *short social exchanges*, even though I can't usually understand enough to keep the conversation going myself.

Fig. 2: European Language Portfolio, Spoken Interaction, levels A1 and A2

The idea that dialogue or conversation is a construction of questions and answers, or merely involves the exchange of information, is very common, but this is definitely not the whole truth. This understanding of dialogue does not provide an authentic picture of what really occurs in dialogue; research in spoken language, genre, pragmatics, and conversation gives us quite a different picture. Information exchange is only one of the fundamental functions of dialogue; Halliday (1985) refers to three main categories of linguistic meta-functions, where one is the information level, which deals with information exchange and semantic content: the *ideational* level. But the picture is incomplete without two other categories, the *textual* and the *interpersonal* meta-functions, the textual level concerning the theme-rheme structure and the interpersonal level fundamentally relating to the relationship between the speakers. This is quite an essential part of normal conversation, but not an essential part of traditional grammar or the traditional understanding of communication as developed by Saussure, whose communicating heads show how the language system resides in the brain of similar-looking individuals without any facial expression, bodies, environment or culture.

During the last ten or fifteen years, research in conversation analysis and discourse analysis has completed this picture.[4] The works of Sacks and Schegloff have, for example, given us new knowledge about the implicit rules or patterns of interaction. These patterns are partly cultural and must be taken into account in foreign language teaching if the goal is communication across cultures. These patterns have also been developed in linguistic politeness research (Brown and Levinson 1987) based on the face work theory of the sociologist Erving Goffman (1967). The notion of politeness is not limited to the polite, well-behaved, almost bourgeois understanding of this concept, but designates the study of how to behave appropriately when interacting with other people in a broader psychological and sociological sense.

The focus on questions and answers in elementary foreign language teaching is also unfortunate because, apart from in the interview genre, this form of interaction is not very frequent without any kind of introduction. Moreover, informal conversation or dialogue is normally accepted as the basic type of linguistic interaction or "the basic form of speech-exchange systems" (Sacks et al. 1978: 47), "Le prototype de toute interaction verbale" (Kerbrat-Orecchioni 1990: 115), whereas the interview genre is actually limited to the media and the courts.

Having established that oral communication in a dialogue is one of the main goals at the beginning level, it might be useful to take a look at what defines authentic dialogue. In her book *La conversation familière* (1996), Véronique Traverso offers an interesting and authentic picture of everyday French conversation between friends and relatives, based on fifteen hours of conversation. A conversation can be divided into main parts: 1) an opening 2) a body 3) a closing, the first part consisting typically of greetings, general flattery or cajolery (amadouage), the second of compliments and comments, and the third part of appreciation, projects, wishes, greetings (Traverso 1996: 225).

It is usually considered a common courtesy in both Denmark and France, as in so many other countries, not to ask questions without any introduction or preparation, both concerning the subject and the interlocutor. The focus on this specific competence in foreign language teaching, while other essential communicative or interaction functions are neglected, is thus quite surprising and inappropriate. This seems nevertheless to be a general problem, as empirically demonstrated by Debrock et al. (1999), who show how Dutch students use mainly questions and answers as their conversation strategy in role plays, thus giving the impression of being too direct, affected and even impolite; their native homologues take up more time, are less direct, contain more discourse markers, and display much more attention to social relations between speakers when it comes to taking turns and initiative in dialogue. These are of course very refined social competences in communication but they are not unfamiliar to learners, who already use such skills in their daily native-speaker interactions.

HANNE LETH ANDERSEN

3. DIALOGUE IN BEGINNERS' TEXTBOOKS

In light of the new focus on communication in legislation from the Danish Ministry of Education, and the contribution made by linguistics and conversation analysis to defining communication, I shall now examine some concrete textbook material. I shall use beginning French textbooks as my data material in order to see how progression and culture are treated in foreign language teaching. Of course, teachers use these textbooks in many different ways, but the material is being used and it is a fairly good indicator of the visions of foreign language teaching. I shall focus on the beginning level for two reasons: first, it is especially in need of input and very often suffers from a focus on grammar that impedes the development of communication skills (Fristrup 2004), and second, I consider culture in and outside language as extremely motivating when it comes to learning languages and therefore find it important to integrate cultural knowledge at the beginning level, not only as something exterior, but as part of the communication – for example, as different ways of interacting, in respect to different social relationships, with forms of politeness, and so forth.

From the above-mentioned political reforms and the focus in the current exam forms, it is quite clear that the skills wanted and tested are oral communication skills, defined as listening comprehension and speaking ability; these are divided into two different skills, both in the *European Language Portfolio* and in *Fremtidens sprogfag* (Fig. 1): at the lower level as proficiency in conversational language use, and at the higher level as proficiency in oral presentations.

How is this achieved in beginners' systems? What is the material like? Are there dialogues and are these authentic?

In order to perceive the actual focus in French language teaching as it is presented in textbooks for beginners, I have chosen to examine two Danish textbooks of French as a foreign language, *Formidable* and *Avant-Garde*, both for use at the primary and lower secondary school level; two textbooks for use at the secondary school level, *Franskbogen* and *Carte Blanche*, and finally a video language-teaching course, *C'est à toi*.

First, I shall take a look at the idea of progression underlying the choice of text material and then at the idea of communication as it is presented in the specific dialogues.

Consulting the tables of content in different textbooks, the authors often appear to have two main focal points: the thematic areas and thus the lexical choices (e.g., for or against nuclear energy, facts about France, a receptionist on the job and at a disco, a presentation of a family, shopping) and the linguistic system: phonetics and grammar (pronunciation of nasal vowels, place of the adjective, the genitive, negation). These two choices merge in one text, especially at the secondary school level. In *Franskbogen* and *Carte Blanche*, grammar is at the center of progression and the tables of content present this as a central point. In *Carte Blanche,* the table of content is divided into four columns, 1) title and length of the different texts (until the above-mentioned reforms, the exam requirements being specified as the number of pages of text offered for an examination), 2) grammar and pronunciation, 3) vocabulary, and 4) information, with a focus on French culture. In *Franskbogen*, we find three columns, parallel to *Carte Blanche*, only vocabulary is distributed between the thematic and grammatical material. The tables in both textbooks function as a description of the vocabulary and the grammatical progression in the book. Since each chapter is clearly connected with a specific content and a grammatical theme, one is lead to believe that the texts are constructed in order to present a specific vocabulary and grammatical information. Lassen (2004) finds that dialogue is important in *Franskbogen* since 49 out of 59 texts are partly or totally dialogues, usually with a presentation of the communication situation. She counts eight types of dialogue in this beginners' textbook, half of them being familiar conversations in the sense of Traverso. Some of the longest texts are interviews, though, with a much simpler structure than certain dialogues earlier in the book, and she argues that the progression is based on an increase in grammatical, not in conversational complexity, since the dialogues early in the book are often much more complex than at a more advanced state (Lassen 2004: 46).

In the textbooks for the primary and lower secondary schools, there is less focus on grammar and we do not find grammar presented explicitly in the tables of content in *Formidable* or *Avant-Garde*. Taking a look at the texts, the progression is much less linear when it comes to grammar, the focus being on listening comprehension with regard to content and on dialogue. It is quite clear though that *Avant-Garde* integrates a much greater number of written texts, whereas the first volume of *Formidable* concentrates almost exclusively on listening comprehension and direct oral production without passing though the written media.

3.2 INTERVIEWS

In the textbooks, dialogue very often means interview. If the interview were the basic genre of communication in the learner's life it would of course make good sense to teach students how to ask questions and to answer. But the interview is not often part of the learner's daily life, except those observed in the media. The interview might however be a good way of getting the learner to speak within a limited semantic area, and sometimes it can be quite authentic. This is the case, for example, when it comes to introducing oneself, as in the typical text "Je m'appelle Nejma" (*Avant-Garde* 1, Students book, 42-43), where the young girl Nejma answers questions about her family posed by an unknown reporter (a drawing in the center of the right-hand page shows a hand with a microphone). A more authentic example of an interview situation may be that of a panel discussion about new family patterns in *Avant Garde* 3: "La famille monoparentale" (Students book, 18-19). In *Franskbogen*, the text "Une interview" presents an interesting example of a journalist being at the center of the text; the journalist, Martine, is at home, calling different women in order to do an interview for a women's magazine. In *Formidable* 2, Textbook (p. 117), the interview, "La chambre de Léo", where two interlocutors talk, one (Vanessa) asking questions about the disposition of young Léo's room, the other (Léo) answering, is hardly authentic, but it does serve the didactic purpose of using the vocabulary of young people's rooms: furniture, colors, books, clothes, roller skates and music systems. The interview is not part of any specific situation; there are no indications of the particular setting, the sequence of events before and after the interview, the relationship between the two interlocutors or their age or personality – there is just Vanessa patiently interrogating Léo about his room.

3.3 DIALOGUE

A dialogue can be based on a question and become a genuine exchange between two persons. In the different textbooks, the settings often present culturally specific scenarios and the persons often represent young French people in typical situations, such as at cafés, at discothèques, at the university restaurant, at school or at home, at the dinner table or doing homework. In addition to the grammatical progression, textbooks usually give great priority to cultural knowledge in the choice of scenarios and persons in the texts. In some, the characters reappear throughout the texts, while in others each text is completely independent. Some texts have an introduction presenting the setting; others start directly with a dialogue, so the learners must figure out the context on their own, in some cases with the help of an illustration.

When it comes to the actual structure of the dialogues, the solutions are very different. Some dialogues consist mainly of questions and answers; some contain the whole situation from the first greeting to the last goodbye, whereas quite a lot introduce the situation and the setting and then give parts of the middle or the body (cf. Traverso 1996) of the dialogue. Some dialogues contain discourse markers, whereas the main function of others seems to be the transmission of information.

Linguistically, the language of some of the dialogues conforms to the characteristics of written language: there is only little actual interaction such as response and feedback and there are few interaction markers in the interlocutors' lines. Didactically, it is interesting to look at the pragmatic functions being realized. Are the learners presented with different ways of interacting other than questions and answers, such as openings of new subjects, theme shifts, expressions of opinion, interest or proposal, and expressions of agreement and disagreement? All these functions are as important as the grammatical knowledge that is often at the centre of the texts.

Most of the dialogues in *Formidable* start *in medias res,* without any introductory text allowing the actual dialogue to be longer. In "L'argent, est-il capital?" (*Formidable* 3, Textbook, 106-107), we find an exchange of opinion between two persons, Sophie and Pierre. The photo accompanying the text shows four young people sitting on a bench in front of a notice board in a small street. Though not evident from the way the text is presented, it is only part of a dialogue, since it must be presumed that the two young people have met, said hello, and somehow started a conversation, just as it does not seem realistic that they stopped quite as abruptly as the dialogue indicates. The last enunciation (*Et la gym alors, … C'est pour qui?*) bears a closer resemblance to the end of a written text, where the last line may very well be a rhetorical punch line, than to the end of a conversation, where, according to Traverso (1996), there will typically be a slowing down phase and some kind of closing mechanism like arrangements and greetings.

HANNE LETH ANDERSEN

The text starts out with Sophie asking Pierre questions, but she then starts expressing opinions and judging his answers: *Là tu as raison. Mais...* The dialogue thus does not consist of only questions and answers, but also reactions to the answers and actual exchanges of opinion between Sophie and Pierre. There may be a large number of questions in this text, but both of the interlocutors ask questions and none of them solely plays the role of interviewer. There is even a theme shift in the middle, with the explicit use of a theme shift expression: *Parlons vêtements maintenant.* This shifter may be very explicit and focused on the meta-level, e.g. "what should we talk about?", but this dialogue has other theme-shifters, like when Pierre returns to a theme from the beginning of the text: *Et toi, alors. L'argent n'est pas du tout important pour toi?*

This text also presents different ways to express disagreement (*Tu rigoles! / Là, tu exagères! / Mais écoute / ..., quand même / Je ne pense pas comme toi / Moi, je trouve ça carrément idiot!*) and agreement (*C'est vrai, d'accord, OK, tu as raison / Tout à fait d'accord*).

Syntactically the text is quite authentic. The full negation (*ne ... pas*) which in everyday spoken French is quite uncommon is not always used, and it is especially avoided with subject pronouns and thus very close to authentic French (Coveney 1998). The word order is straightforward and nominal subjects are only used alone very few times, as in everyday spoken French (Jeanjean 1981, Andersen 1999). When it comes to questions, these follow what we know about question formation in spoken French: *Est-ce que* is used to introduce a new theme in the beginning of the text, and later to change the angle of a discussion, introduced by *mais* (*Mais est-ce que c'est nécessaire de suivre la mode?*). There are elliptic questions, referring naturally back to former enunciations (*Comment ça? / Quoi par exemple*), questions with infinitives (*Pourquoi porter un T-shirt Calvin Klein ou Nike?*), and full uninverted yes-no questions (*Et pour ça, il faut de l'argent?*), three of which are naturally underlined by *non* or *hein* (*Mais on peut voir les copains chez soi, non? / Il faut quand-même des vêtements, non? / On veut s'habiller comme tout le monde, hein?*). We may conclude that this dialogue is rather authentic in its structure and syntax. There are topic shifts using explicit topic shifters, discussion, opinions, and the syntax follows the rules of standard spoken French.

The text entitled "Amitié" (*Formidable* 3, Textbook, 74-75), however, may look like a dialogue, in that it consists exclusively of direct quotes, but there is no real interaction between the interlocutors. It is structured like a short thesis about the specific subject/theme of 'friendship'. First comes a definition of the notion of friendship (hypothesis), after which it is compared to good fellowship (antithesis), and then the third main part defines the qualities to be expected in a good friend (synthesis). The text contains a conclusion presenting the last rhetorical punch line: *Je ne pourrais pas vivre sans amis.* In all, this gives us three major parts, divided by shorter parts containing a small personal question from Anne to Hugo. This is also typographically motivated, since otherwise the text would look very monotonous with one-line remarks all the way through. Anne asks the questions and is in charge of the dialogue, almost without reacting to the answers, and she is also the one who presents her own opinion and the conclusion at the end. This is not amazing for the interview genre but is very far from the dialogue it tends to look like, not only in the way it is set up typographically but also due to the photo accompanying the text, which might also lead one to think of a friendly, informal conversation rather than a clearly planned interview.

The text has none of the ingredients we have seen in Traverso (1996): no opening, no closing, no topic shifts, no discussion, no disagreement, and almost no reaction on Anne's part to Hugo's answers. The dialogue seems like a pretence for writing a text on a specific subject, and the interlocutors never resemble actual people with opinions. This of course explains why they cannot disagree, but rather only confirm each other's opinions: *Tu as tout à fait raison* and *Je suis d'accord – à cent pour cent.*

The syntax is very close to that of authentic spoken French as regards the form of the questions, word order and pronouns. This is supported by the lexical choices – for example, the use of 'nanas' and 'sympa' – yet at the same time both of the young people also unhesitatingly make use of several abstract nouns to describe friends (*Franchise … générosité … patience … sensibilité … […] confiance et tolérance*), despite the fact that in standard spoken French the norm is to use verbal expressions, final verbs and predicative adjectives in descriptions (Halliday 1985, Koch 1995): *ils sont francs, ils sont génereux, patients …* This actually occurs in the first definition of a friend at the beginning of the text, which consists of an indefinite noun followed by the neutral pronoun *ce* (*Un ami, c'est très solide* and *un copain c'est plus superficiel*).

The only place in the text where Hugo hesitates when confronted with Anne's questions is when he is asked to define good fellowship;

HANNE LETH ANDERSEN

here he starts with *eh ben*. It might be more natural for him to hesitate when confronted with the girl's question about what the boys talk about when they are alone, but in this situation he answers at once, telling her that they talk about girls and sex. It might also be expected that he would hesitate when faced with more abstract questions, like when he is asked to describe qualities of friends.

In *Franskbogen*, the dialogues are usually introduced by a few lines presenting the situation and the interlocutors. There are many daily life situations such as "Au restau-U" (*Franskbogen*, 32), where we find an example of what might actually be a whole dialogue between two young people meeting at a university restaurant, from greetings to the young man's invitation and the young woman's evasive answer: "peut-être". Before the dialogue, one of the interlocutors, Anne-Marie, a young Danish girl, is introduced. She finds herself at the university restaurant for the first time and is eager to find an empty chair. The dialogue starts when she has found one at David's table. The dialogue is short, with greetings, presentations, an invitation, and a polite rejection using "je regrette"; it also contains the interactive function of the reactive response "ah bon!".

The title of the dialogue "Pour ou contre la CEE" (*Franskbogen*, 58) announces an opposition of opinions, and this is also what the text deals with; but there are few actual linguistic markers of disagreement between the two interlocutors, Christophe and Lars, and only two opinion markers: *moi je pense que, je suis contre*... The two young men clearly don't agree, but the exchange of opinion has no actual introduction, beginning or end. After Lars's last turn, a short text explains that Lars has only been in France for two months and therefore he has difficulty expressing his arguments. The text represents a cultural encounter and the two young men's opinions are well in line with typical French and typical Danish opinions about the European Community. As a didactic text, however, it poorly expresses the pragmatic functions that would normally be linked with disagreement, and most striking is the fact that there is absolutely no representation of the politeness strategies that are often associated with disagreement in conversation such as indirectness: *in a way, slightly* or *maybe*, or pre-sequences (Jackson & Jacobs): *you might not agree with me in this, but...*; *yes, you are right, but still...* or *I understand what you are saying, but...*

4. THE INTERPERSONAL META-FUNCTION

Dialogues in beginners' textbooks are often not authentic dialogues in either a structural or pragmatic sense; they are constructed to ensure that grammar and vocabulary can be presented and practiced. Dialogue texts often lack opening and closing sequences, focusing instead on the middle sequence, the informative part of authentic dialogue, which leaves less room or time for the interpersonal parts. The exchanges in the dialogues take place mainly through the use of questions and answers.

This didactic choice is a combination of the classical idea that progression is based on explicit grammatical knowledge and the just as classical focus on the information level of language to the detriment of the interpersonal function. Splitting up a text into lines of speech makes it suitable for reading aloud, and this of course offers the opportunity to work on emphasis and intonation. But it is important to stress that this kind of pronunciation training easily turns into pronunciation rules in the interface between writing and speaking, into decoding the relation between letters and sounds, which for the French language is an extremely complicated affair, instead of going directly from the perception of sounds to their production (Andersen 1998). Fortunately, beginners' systems today are often accompanied by CDs with the sound track of the textbook, which makes it possible for the learner to ignore the disturbing image of the words when training pronunciation.

The extremely low priority given to the interpersonal level in textbooks is also apparent in the often unclear relationship between the interlocutors in the dialogue, which makes it unrealistic and one dimensional and, consequently, uninteresting to the students; specified relationships and culturally specific actions might make the dialogues more dynamic.

It is also quite unrealistic that the interlocutors repeatedly ask questions without preparatory phrases. Asking questions is potentially face threatening (Brown & Levinson, Sacks & Schlegloff) and demands some degree of preparation. Some of the dialogues we have seen are based on agreement and therefore signal more distance and politeness than disagreement would.[5] But then again, some cultures favour agreement more than others; according to cultural theory, the Danish culture, for example, is a consensus culture whereas the French focuses more on involvement (Hampden-Turner & Trompenaars 1997) or vehemence (d'Iribarne 1989).

HANNE LETH ANDERSEN

The *Amitié* dialogue is based on agreement whereas the *Argent* dialogue integrates a good deal of discussion and exchange of opinion. In this way the relationship between the interlocutors is given, since according to Sacks and Schegloff's theory about adjacency pairs, the preferred reaction to an utterance is agreement, just as the preferred and unmarked reaction to a request is acceptance.[6] After a rejection, just like after any other non-preferred reaction, there will almost always be a pause or a hesitation, followed by a justification. The *Amitié* dialogue focuses on agreement, which suggests that the two people do not know each other very well, and it is all the more surprising to see Hugo's willing and precise answers even to Anne's personal questions. If Danish language learners used this form of dialogue when meeting French people, even young people, it would be considered face threatening and as a violation of the conventions of politeness.

The *Argent* dialogue is less personal, but the form of the discussion indicates that the two young people know each other better, and there is a closer connection between the form and the semantic content (ideational level), the interpersonal relations and the face work.

In order to improve learners' communicative competence, dialogues in beginners' textbooks might focus more on the structure of authentic dialogue and integrate more opening and closing sequences, more topic shifters and more techniques for exchanging opinions; in short, there is a need for an increased focus on the relational function of language and conversation. Considering the people and situations jointly would thus create more authenticity and give learners improved tools for communication and a better understanding of interaction markers and interaction patterns, whether general or specific to one language or culture.

5. CONCLUSION

Clearly, interaction is important in the composition of foreign language textbooks. Many textbook chapters are presented as conversations between two or three people. Some are interviews; others are presented as dialogues. But authentic dialogue between interlocutors does not just involve exchanging information, asking questions and giving answers. Along with the grammatical input that is often the focus of the progression of textbook, the many pragmatic and interpersonal functions must also be included if the goal is communicative competence.

From examples of dialogue in French textbooks for beginners we have seen that they often provide material that focuses on sentence structure rather than the structure of dialogue. A focus on vocabulary must include not only the vocabulary of the various themes studied, but also the vocabulary of interpersonal exchange, discourse markers or gambits. If such linguistic features are not present in dialogue text, they will not be easily integrated in the learners' language and their language will be too full of information and ultimately impolite. Textbook dialogues cannot be authentic dialogues, but they can integrate specific rules of politeness and thus be a better example of culture in language than is sometimes the case.

The idea of progression in language learning should not let go of the grammatical focus, but it can integrate a more or less implicit grammatical dimension in more realistic dialogues that concentrate on interpersonal exchanges. If learners are to become more competent in communicating, as recommended and required by the new reforms of the primary and lower secondary school and the secondary school, they must be introduced to different types of dialogue including opening and closing sequences and interpersonal exchanges. Language teaching must give priority to the relational functions of language and not only to the referential function; the exchange of information may be the main focus in written language, but this is not the case in oral communication.

NOTES

1 Author's translation from Danish.
2 http://www.faelles maal.uvm.dk/fag
3 "Anvende grundlæggende franske høfligheds- og omgangsformer; Anvende ofte forekommende faste vendinger og kulturbundne udtryk" (*Trinmål for fransk*, http://www.faellesmaal.uvm.dk/fag/Fransk/trinmaal_synoptisk.html).
4 While conversation analysis takes it point of departure in sociology, discourse analysis is part of the linguistic paradigm. Its goal is to use the principles of linguistic analysis on larger entities than the sentence. In addition, conversation analysis is mainly preoccupied with oral conversation, whereas discourse analysis also deals with written texts.
5 "Il est souvent admis qu'une règle implicite de la conversation est la préférence pour l'accord puisque c'est un type d'interaction dans lequel les participants cherchent avant tout à confirmer leur relation et leurs représentations d'eux-mêmes et des autres" (Traverso 1996: 165).
6 Other adjacency pairs are greeting-greeting, question-answer, offer-acceptance/rejection, request-acceptance/rejection.

BIBLIOGRAPHY

Andersen, H.L. 1999. 'Subjektets plads i ikke-spørgende sætninger på spontant talt fransk', *Ny Forskning i Grammatik, Fællespublikation* 6 (23-39).

– 1998. 'Talesprog og begynderundervisning', *Fransk Nyt* 217, 33-39.

Brown, P. & S.C. Levinson 1987. *Politeness: some universals in language usage*, Cambridge: Cambridge University Press.

Coveney, A. 1998. 'Awareness of linguistic constraints on variable *ne* omission'. In: *Journal of French Language Studies* 8, 159-187.

Debrock, M. & D. Flament-Boistrancourt & R. Gevaert 1999. 'Le manque de 'naturel' des interactions verbales du non-francophone en français. Analyse de quelques aspects à partir du corpus LANCOM', *Faits de Langues* 13, Paris: Ophrys, 46-56.

D'Iribarne, P. 1989. *La logique de l'honneur: Gestion des entreprises et traditions nationales*. Paris: Editions du Seuil.

Fremtidens sprogfag, Uddannelsesstyrelsens Temahæfteserie no. 5, 2003.

Fristrup, D. 2004. 'Grammatik i franskundervisningen – en empirisk undersøgelse', In: *(Pré)publications* 190, 77-96.

Goffman, E. 1967. 'On face work', In: *Interaction Ritual*. Chicago: Aldine, 5-45.

Halliday, M.A.K. 1985. *An Introduction to Functional Grammar*. London: Edward Arnold.

Hampden-Turner, C. & F. Trompenaars 1997. *Riding the Waves of Culture, Understanding Diversity in Global Business*. New York: McGraw-Hill.

Jackson, S. & S. Jacobs 1978. *Adjacency pairs and the sequential description of arguments*. Paper presented at the annual convention of The Speech Communication Association, Minneapolis.

Kerbrat-Orecchioni, C. 1990-1992-1994. *Les interactions verbales*, 1 à 3, Paris: Armand Colin.

Koch, P. 1995. 'Subordination, intégration syntaxique et 'oralité', *La subordination dans les langues romanes, Etudes Romanes* 34, University of Copenhagen.

Lassen, H. 2004. *Hvor er samtalen i dialogen?*, Kandidatspeciale, Afdeling for Klassisk og Romansk, Aarhus Universitet.

Sacks, H. 1975. 'Tout le monde doit mentir', *Communications* 20, 182-203.

Sacks, H., E. Schegloff & G. Jefferson 1974. 'A simplist systematics for the organization of turn-taking for conversation', in J. Schenkein (ed.), 1978: *Studies in the Organisation of Conversational Interaction*. London: Academic Press, 7-57.

Schegloff, E. 1980. 'Preliminaries to preliminaries: Can I ask you a question', *Sociological Inquiry* 50, 104-152.

Traverso, V. 1996. *La conversation familière*. Lyon: Presses Universitaires de Lyon.

Beginners' Textbooks

Formidable, M. Brandelius & I. Sundell, Danish edition: Leon Aktor, Forlag Alinea.

Avant Garde, E. Kambskard, B. Brandt-Nilsson & D. Eychenne, Forlag Malling Beck.

Franskbogen, V. Gade, Forlag Systime.

Carte Blanche, J. Fitzner & T. Rhein-Knudsen, Forlag Kaleidoscope.

Video

C'est à toi, Forlag Alinea.

Film Dialogue as a Resource for Promoting Language Awareness

Francesco Caviglia

Abstract

Helping learners rise from an implicit to an explicit and more mature under-standing of language and communication is a challenging issue for educational intervention in language learning. This paper suggests that film dialogue – which is carefully crafted to sound 'natural', but avoids the idiosyncrasies and 'noise' of real-life conversation – can be a viable option as a model of language, and also as a catalyser of classroom activities based on analysis and discussion of language choices as they are recognizable in the spoken version of the dialogue and in the subtitles.

The proposed examples highlight the tight connection of language and culture, and the need for taking advantage of the pragmatic competence acquired by adult learners in their mother tongue.

1. INTRODUCTION: BACKGROUND ASSUMPTIONS, INSPIRING PRINCIPLES

This paper suggests that film dialogue may be a valuable resource for helping students develop *language awareness*. After a brief discussion of the role of *language awareness* in the process of language learning, I shall present examples of classroom and language lab activities designed on the premise that dialogue in film can provide a good language model for activities aimed at making knowledge about language more explicit. Working with language in films is today a feasible option for classrooms since digital video has become relatively inexpensive and easy to view and manipulate. For those who wish to put the ideas presented in this paper into practice, technical details are available as an appendix.

1.1 EXPLICIT KNOWLEDGE ABOUT LANGUAGE AS A RESOURCE AND AS AN INSTRUCTIONAL PROBLEM

In their everyday life, adults can adapt their language and behaviour to different contexts and needs, on the basis of a typically implicit knowledge of and ability to use a variety of tools and strategies, such as specific communicative acts (greetings, offers, refusals, acceptances, apologies...), politeness as mutual face-saving strategy, context-dependent variability in language and action, discursive construction of social identities and relations. There is also evidence that adults try more or less consciously to apply this universal pragmatic competence when they learn a second language (Kasper & Rose 2002: 164-167).

On these premises, second language learning would benefit from educational intervention on two interrelated but separate issues:

- bringing the learner's knowledge about language and communication from implicit to explicit;
- enabling the learner to notice and understand specific features of the target language.

Educational intervention on these two fronts ought therefore to make the learner able to speak of language and communication and thereby foster *language awareness* as "development in learners of an enhanced consciousness of and sensibility to the forms and functions of language" (Carter 2003). *Language awareness* suggests educational focus on *intentional learning* (Bereiter & Scardamalia 1989) and is a key ingredient of adult, *advanced* literacy (Caviglia 2004).

Linguists concerned with language awareness often focus on producing descriptions of language that may serve educators (White 2000: 91). This paper focuses instead on aspects of instructional design, in an effort to overcome a recurring problem with explicit instruction on language:

- when talking about language, the student is often on shaky ground on both language and meta-language (e.g., talking about syntax structures in L2);
- when meta-language is taught as a subject matter – which usually occurs within a mother tongue curriculum – the student (or even the teacher) is seldom confronted with problems she or he perceives as concrete and challenging.

In order to obviate this problem, the following ingredients would seem to be required:

FRANCESCO CAVIGLIA

- a 'language playground', that is an environment where the students (and maybe the teacher) work within their *zone of proximal development* on understanding how language and communication work;
- tools for observing and manipulating language;
- questions and activities which require the noticing of – and eventually the understanding of –relevant features of language and communication by processing both language and meta-language;
- explicit integration of L1 and L2 competences.

Film dialogue is the catalyser for integrating these ingredients into educational intervention aimed at fostering language awareness.

1.2 FILM DIALOGUE AS MODEL LANGUAGE

From the point of view of language teaching, it could be assumed that everyday conversation was the only discursive genre whereby adult or young adult participants in a language class could discuss on almost equal footing with the teacher. They may lack the meta-language or they may not fully understand the target language, but they should be able to produce and understand nuances of language at a level adequate to at least one *languacultural* environment in which they have been socialized (Bialystock 1993; Risager 2003 and this volume, for the concept of *languaculture*). So, if the educational goal is 'language awareness', why not use everyday speech as the 'language playground' of choice?

Indeed, the oral language in conversation is a highly regarded topic in the study of language and culture. At the most general level, everyday speech is considered as containing the primary genres from which all other discursive genres have derived (Bakhtin 1986: 60-62; Todorov 1984: 81-82). As for the learning and teaching of languages, the analysis of oral corpora is a key source of insight into which language features are actually used by native speakers (see Andersen this volume, for an analysis of the educational implications).

Unfortunately, unprepared conversation is an impractical object to deal with in a classroom: transcripts of conversation show how natural speech is full of noise, self-corrections and mistakes. Moreover, recordings of everyday speech are often boring to listen to, since private conversation is not designed – at least in principle – for the entertainment of outsiders.

From the point of view of language learning and teaching, film dialogue may therefore provide a better option as model language and as a source of questions aimed at developing language awareness. Of course, film dialogue is by no means *authentic*; however, it is carefully *constructed* for the benefit of the viewer by a team of well-paid professionals (screenwriters, directors, actors, cameramen) whose task is to make it *ring* true, spontaneous, and entertaining: a kind of peer-reviewed spoken language bestowed with features which make it especially suited to become a model of communication in a language learning classroom. For example, film dialogue

- is designed and staged for the benefit of an external viewer (Rossi, 2002: 163), which implies that all auditive and visual means are employed to create *context* which should motivate and ease understanding;
- has more coherence and cohesion and less 'noise' (hesitations, self-corrections...) than real-life conversation (Rossi 2002: 174-175);
- is bound to reflect the language norm within a given milieu.

Moreover, the language and appearance of the characters who take part in a film have to be socio-culturally recognizable by the viewer (more on this point below, in the examples). In other words, film dialogue is a sort of *distilled speech* occurring in situations rich in context and culture, as suggested by Kramsch (1996) to create an ideal setting for the learning of language and culture. To all these reasons, digital video technology adds the possibility of observing and even manipulating film dialogue with unprecedented ease.

1.3 DIGITAL VIDEO AND SUBTITLES AS RESOURCES FOR OBSERVING LANGUAGE

A simple change of the physical support, from tape to DVD or computer file, makes it now possible to access instantly a single scene and 'jump' from one location of the film to another. This development has made video – for the first time – into an object *almost* as flexible as a printed book, and therefore usable as an everyday tool for the average learner and teacher.

Given the pivotal role that subtitles play in some of the examples proposed below, a few words are devoted here to features which are relevant to language learning and language observing activities.

Subtitles are called *interlingual* when one language is spoken on the screen and another one – typically the viewer's mother tongue – is used in the subtitles. Interlingual subtitles are not a literal translation of what is said on the screen, but have to capture "the gist" of the dialogue within severe constraints of time and space (Wildblood 2002: 1). This implies that subtitles are more compact than a translation of the film transcript, but should convey the same emotions to the viewer: good subtitles may therefore be quite creative (de Linde 1995; Card 1998; Nornes 1999).

The same freedom is not enjoyed by *intralingual* subtitles (sometimes called 'close captions'), that is the subtitles written for hearing impaired and for second language learners (the latter could indeed be regarded as partially phoneme-deaf). Intralingual subtitles should represent (almost) full duplication of the language of the soundtrack (Jung 1990), as far as the space and time constraints make it possible. This seems to be the general rule for English, French and Danish films, seen from my non-native speaker's viewpoint. In the case of Italian intralingual subtitles, however, striking differences between the audio and the subtitles are not uncommon, as discussed in some of the examples below.

Intralingual subtitles, be they 'faithful' to the original spoken word to a greater or lesser degree, are especially interesting for work on language awareness in both L2 and L1. First of all, they duplicate the keywords of the dialogue, thereby offering in the first place a powerful help to understand the dialogue (in L2 learning) and then providing a useful reminder which stays on the screen when a scene is analysed in classroom situations. Besides, the possible lack of correspondence between the spoken and the written word is the result of choices that are worth being understood and discussed.

Finally, I wish to mention that students need not be regarded only as viewers of subtitles; advanced or even intermediate learners can also, with relative ease, write inter- and intra-lingual subtitles themselves, thereby providing yet another source of problems and questions to be examined in the classroom (see appendix for some technical details on subtitling).

2. OBSERVING AND DISCUSSING FILM DIALOGUE: SOME EXAMPLES

In the learning activity described below in this section, a class visions a film scene and then holds discussions – first in small groups and then collectively – in order to find answers to one or more questions provided by the teacher. The students, on the basis of their own understanding of language and communication, and with only minimal help from the teacher, are expected to find acceptable answers to the questions. The activity is aimed at letting the class rise above *implicit understanding* of communication, but also at making clear to the students that they *do* understand much about language and communication, but that a more specific vocabulary and the acquisition of some conceptual tools would make the discussion more productive.

The proposals described below can usually be completed within a 45 minutes period. The examples presented have first been tried out with Danish university students of Italian and with Danish and Italian teachers of Italian; they are also currently being tried out with Italian secondary school students (aged 14 to 16) within an Italian mother tongue curriculum.

2.1 FACE WORK

Recognizing the function of communication as a means not only to 'transmit' contents, but also to construct relationships and identities (Fairclough and Wodak 1997) is one important step for advancing from a referential view of language to one considering communication as a purposive act designed to establish and fine-tune a relationship (Tannen 1989, 1992 and 1997) or, in more general terms, to enter a dialogue with the Other (Bakhtin 1986; Todorov 1984).

A scene which can introduce this idea of communication – and also shows how power relationships can define a rigid (but not always unbreakable) frame to communication, is the first dialogue between Lacombe Lucien and Mr. Horn in Louis Malle's *Lacombe Lucien* (1974). Lucien is a poor, rural and uneducated French teenager who becomes a member of the German police in 1944 in order to get some status. He becomes involved in extorting money and gratis clothes from Mr. Horn, a wealthy Jewish tailor from Paris who is now living in hiding in the province. The first time Lucien visits Mr. Horn alone to collect his new suit (the *first* real suit Lucien will own), the young man is clearly intimidated, but also aware that the balance of power is in his favour. The scene is almost comical in the beginning, with Lucien embarrassed over having to take off his trousers but nevertheless finding some relief in the revolver that he can place on a shelf as evidence of his role. Mr. Horn treats him with the discrete politeness he would use if Lucien were one of his rich former clients, an adequate solution at first sight for both of them to save face by hiding their condition of blackmailer and victim. Mr. Horn tries to engage Lucien in small-talk about clothes, but Lucien does not even have the vocabulary for the topic. Mr. Horn decides then to ask Lucien about his interests and activities, clearly meaning his activities *prior to* being a collaborator. But Lucien's previous life of poverty and humiliation is not something he wants to talk about, and the question prompts him to set the tailor straight about their relationship and to retort "I am a member of the German police". In order to reinforce his position, Lucien adds "Mr. Jean-Bernard [Lucien's mentor in the militia and the person who sent him to collect money from the tailor] dit que les Juifs sont les ennemis de la France" [M. Jean-Bernard says that the Jews are the enemies of France], to which Mr. Horn answers "Non, pas moi" [No, I am not]. A long silence follows, after which Mr. Horn's daughter appears on the screen, and Lucien and the public discover that her name is… France.

Learners from the age of 14 up are quite capable of understanding the logic behind the verbal and gestural behaviour of both: how both try first of all to save face, how Lucien only becomes aggressive when he feels threatened by the risk that his own social and cultural inferiority would betray him; how Mr. Horn clings to the routine of the tailor-client relationship; finally, how it is an element external to the dialogue, the daughter's name, that confirms to Lucien and to the viewer that indeed the tailor is by no means an enemy of the French state and people. The most sensitive students are also able to recognize how Lucien's aggressiveness is slightly curbed by the fact that he presents the accusation "Jews are the enemies of France" as coming from a third (although authoritative) person and not from Lucien himself: this leaves to Mr. Horn room for contradicting Lucien in a matter-of-fact tone ('Non, pas moi') which poses a lesser threat to the young man's self-esteem.

Once the students manage to make their understanding of this scene explicit, they are able to appreciate Goffman's (1959) theorisation of the constraints framing human interaction: saving one's *face* and avoiding threatening the other's face by following a *line* of behaviour which minimizes the risks. It may become necessary to change line if the interaction takes unexpected turns, as it happens in most of the interactions between Mr. Horn and Lucien throughout the whole film.

Recognizing *face-work* as a ruling principle in human interaction is a crucial step for introducing the concept of *politeness* (Brown & Levinson, 1987) as a language universal with quite different language- and culture-specific traits, an example of which is proposed in the following paragraph.

2.2 INDIRECTNESS

Lydia, female character in the comedy *Sliding doors* (1998) reproaches her lover, who had failed to understand a wish of hers: "I'm a woman. We don't say what we want but we do reserve the right to get pissed off when we don't get it."

This quote comes in handy to introduce how requests are especially face-threatening acts, which therefore are usually softened by some form of *indirectness*. Tannen ([1986]1992: 16-17) suggests looking at conversation as a system governed by intrinsically conflicting goals, namely: showing affection and keeping independence, obtaining what we want without imposing ourselves. Tannen further explains that not being explicit is also a way of making one's message more emotionally involving for the partner:

> It is a tenet of education that students understand information better, perhaps only, if they have discovered it by themselves rather than being told it. Much as one cares *for* a person, animal, place, or object that one has taken care *of*, so listeners and readers not only understand information better but care more about it – understand it *because* they care about it – if they have worked to make its meaning. (Tannen 1989: 17, emphasis in the original)

This idea is exemplified in the next example, taken from a recent Italian comedy (*L'ultimo bacio* [The last kiss], 2001). A pregnant woman is making plans for the future with her soon-to-be husband and asks him:

> Amore, e se ci comprassimo una casa tutta nostra invece che stare qui in affitto? [Dear, what if we bought our own house, instead of paying rent?] *Italian subtitles*: Potremmo comprare una casa, invece di stare in affitto [we could buy a house, instead of paying rent]

The man looks bewildered at her and answers

Eh?
Italian subtitles: Come? [What?]

I asked the students to rephrase the same request which the woman makes in various forms, from more to less direct. The students (both Danish and Italian) immediately identified the original spoken version as ingeniously indirect and proposed at the opposite pole sentences equivalent to "I wish us to buy our own house, instead of paying rent". Assuming this last sentence as the referential meaning of the sentence, I asked the students to identify the linguistic devices used to make the request easier to accept, or even to refuse. At the same time, I asked how much indirectness had been lost in the Italian subtitles.

Firstly, the form used for the request "E se" + conjunctive (roughly equivalent to a "What if") is probably the most general and non-committing available option for making a request or proposal. The object to be bought is made more attractive by being emphatically described as "una casetta tutta nostra" [a small house of our own]. The man is addressed in an intimate manner as "Amore" ["my love", "my dear"]. Most of these nuances go lost in the subtitles, where the request is reformulated into "Perché non…" [why not…], which retains a lower level of indirectness by implying that the speaker expects a positive answer.

Reasons of brevity were obviously a motive behind the choice of a more compact language in the subtitles. However, the slightly impolite "Eh?" uttered by the reluctant husband has been reformulated into a more acceptable "Come?" [What?]; in other words, brevity was not the most overriding concern: compliance with the rules of the written code also played a role; more on this point below.

On one occasion, after all the above-mentioned elements had been recognized by the students, one of the students – not casually, a young woman – challenged the assumption that the sentence was primarily a request for buying a house. She pointed out that the woman wanted first of all a sign of commitment from her fiancé, and that the house was only the *apparent* target. Other female students added that this was *obvious* and that only men could be so deaf as not to recognize it from the beginning!

Swearing is a topic which requires good *languacultural* sensitivity by L2 learners and teachers. The goal of the following example is to point out the communicative function(s) of swearing, as well as the fact that rude language too must obey rules.

In the example, a gorgeous young woman (she is 18, but we don't know it yet) is flirting with a 10-year-older man she has just met at a party (by the way, the man is the reluctant husband we just encountered). The two are introducing themselves; the man has just mentioned that he works in advertising. Now it is the girl's turn, and in her reply she makes a rude, disparaging allusion to the high school she is still attending.

> Lo sai che io voglio fare l'attrice? Appena finisco *'sto cazzo di liceo* mi iscrivo a una scuola di recitazione. [my emphasis; You know, I want to be an actress. After I finish fucking high school, I'll go to an acting school]. *Italian subtitles*: Io voglio fare l'attrice. Finito il liceo, m'iscrivo a recitazione. [*English subtitles*: I want to be an actress. After high school, I'll go to an acting school.]

Why does the girl make an allusion of this kind? Does she hate her school? And why is the swearword not reported in the subtitles? Isn't it *relevant*?

Neither the Danish, nor the Italian students had any difficulty in recognizing that the main issue for the girl was distancing herself from her condition of teenager, which made her an inappropriate partner for a man of about 30. The derogative allusion to the school was a way of saying that she was already out of school… virtually, which does not necessarily imply that she hated her school: here the Italian students had a good point in maintaining that her *tone* did not contain any hostility towards the high school (a few seemed more than happy to demonstrate how the same sentence could have been expressed differently, so as to *really* convey distaste). The Danish students also felt that although the girl was probably not that enthusiastic about her school, the use of this swearword did not necessarily mean that she hated it. However, their conclusion was based on their understanding of the situation rather than of the tone used by the girl.

A few Italian students were of the opinion that swearing meant nothing in that context; it was just a *normal* way for young people to refer to their school. This idea had soon to be refined, however, as *that* way of referring to one's school could only be considered a standard when teenagers speak with each other and not in the presence of adults with whom they are not in confidence. And, for different reasons, not everybody would have used that vulgar expression in similar circumstances. In addition, neither the (potentially) bad-mouthed nor others would have needed to *think* before using or not using the word.

The choice by the Italian and the English subtitlers not to translate the swearword was at first acknowledged by the students as reasonable, since the word has no referential value. On the other hand, the word *is* relevant and even *realistic*, in that context. However, when we figured out (with the Italian students) what the subtitles would look like with the addition of the swearword, many noticed that the written sentence on the screen would appear far more vulgar than the same words uttered in a matter-of-fact tone by an angelic blond, as in the film.

This last observation introduced the issue of the complex relationship between the spoken and the written word, two aspects which are dealt with in the following sections. For further classroom activity on bad language in a multi-language perspective *Stand by me* (1986), a story based on four male teenagers living a dramatic adventure together, offers a mine of *equivalence* problems (as described, e.g., in Card 1998) and a way to see them solved differently in the subtitles and in other languages used for synchronization.[1]

2.4 SOCIO-CULTURAL IDENTITY IN LANGUAGE

In Italy all foreign films are dubbed into a language that is devoid of the regional marks which are almost always present in the 'true' spoken Italian (Rossi 1999b).

Maybe also for the sake of distinguishing themselves from imported products, Italian films – especially comedies – usually portrait characters with a well-defined geographical and social outcome. These traits need to be identifiable at first sight for the Italian viewer, without jeopardizing the general understanding of what the characters say (a discussion in Rossi 1999a: 79-86). As a result of these constraints, a 'standard Italian' ('Italiano dell'uso medio' in Sabatini 1985) sprayed with a few marked expressions is the preferred solution in most recent commercial films, while films for a niche-public often provide more realistic language solutions, which may be perceived as excessive or simply not understandable by the average viewer.

Recognizing the socio-cultural marks in film language is therefore important for intermediate and advanced learners of L2 Italian, since these marks are relevant for understanding and appreciating films; for native speakers – who are supposed to have no trouble recognizing these marks – it would be desirable to understand how a language which sounds 'realistic' to the ear is indeed the result of a deliberate choice to highlight some given traits.

In the archetypal Italian comedy *I soliti ignoti* [the usual unknowns] (1956), a bunch of small-time crooks gathers to make a coup. Among them is Michele, whom the viewer – before even meeting him in person – knows comes from Sicily where he keeps his sister Carmela (a typical South-Italian name) locked in the house. When two other members of the gang ring the door bell, the sister wakes him up with the words "Michele, bussarono" [Michele, there is someone at the door; lit. "they knocked"]. The use of a simple past (*passato remoto*) instead of the standard compound form "hanno bussato" confirms that Michele and Carmela come from Sicily. The viewer is then given plenty of reminders of their Sicilian background in the following scene, in which Michele – who looks and talks like a prototypical Sicilian – makes it plain that his first priority and concern in life is his sister's *honour*. In order just to be able to *see* Michele's sister (she is not allowed outside), another member of the gang then has the idea of ringing the door bell and pretending to be her brother Michele, who rings because he has forgotten his key. To this end, he feigns a nasal accent and says: "Sono Michele, dimenticai la chiave" [it's Michele, I forgot the key; again, *simple past*]

Oddly, the subtitles *translate* the simple past "bussarono" and "dimenticai" into past perfect, thereby hiding their Sicilian trait and the role it plays in the story. This example might be liquidated as just unfortunate subtitling, but is not an exception. In a hugely popular TV-series the protagonist *commissario* Montalbano, a detective from Sicily, presents himself countless times on the phone as "Montalbano sono" [I am Montalbano], while 'standard Italian' would require "sono" [I am] followed by the caller's name. "Montalbano sono" has become a sort of trademark and even stands as a heading on a web-site for fans of the commissar. But again, the subtitles for hearing-impaired people normalize it into "Sono Montalbano", a colourless sentence no reader would ever find in the novels by Andrea Camilleri on which the TV-series is based.

Why is subtitling in these cases so different from the spoken word?

Subtitlers have slightly different policies about respect for the language norm, in case the original soundtrack is perceived as *deviant*. Ivarsson & Carroll (1998: 157) are adamant that "the language should be (grammatically) 'correct' since subtitles serve as a model for literacy"; Kovačič (1996) suggests instead more willingness on the side of the subtitlers to put the language norm in discussion. The presence of regional marks (that is, of language features that are not plain *substandard*) adds another factor to consider. There is little doubt that hiding the Sicilian traits in the above mentioned examples of subtitles was unfortunate, especially if we consider that the spoken sentences were by no means *wrong*, but other cases are less clear-cut. A typical language mark of people from Rome speaking Italian with a regional and popular accent is the dropping of the last syllable in infinitives: 'mangiare' [to eat] thus becomes *mangia'*. Should the subtitles make this (both local *and* substandard) trait *visible* or should they normalize it into standard Italian? Answering this question requires the students to *notice* language features and discuss them in a situation which is less artificial than most typical classroom activity. Even better, with L1 students, would be moving from discussing subtitles to developing alternative ones, especially for the benefit of L2 students (see appendix for the technical aspects): L1 students would have no difficulties in decoding the spoken words and would be able to concentrate on the most appropriate solutions for rendering them in written form, thereby developing a better understanding of both the written and the oral code.[2]

The issue of oral vs. written language is further discussed in the examples below, in which the regional variant is zeroed, thereby leaving more room for focusing on the language norm in more general terms.

2.5 WRITTEN VS. SPOKEN LANGUAGE: DISCUSSING THE LANGUAGE NORM

The main goal with the examples in this section is to show – once again using conflicts between the spoken word and the subtitles for triggering observation – that language is not just a matter of norms, but also of choices. The examples I am proposing focus on formulations which are absolutely standard as oral language but may cause a raised brow if seen in print:

* *topic-comment* sentence structure;
* sentences starting with a conjunction.

In the already mentioned comedy *L'ultimo bacio* (2001), one character utters a sentence containing what can be regarded as the main message that the film sends to the viewer:

> E' la normalità, la vera rivoluzione ['Normality is the true revolution' or: 'the true revolution, it is normality']

This sentence becomes in the subtitles "La vera rivoluzione è la normalità". Both sentences are correct by any standard and have almost the same length (the original would just require one extra comma).

In another recent film (*La meglio gioventù* [the best of youth], 2003), the protagonist talks to a young woman, whom we have just heard playing classic piano, and we hear that she is studying maths at the university. This prompts him to ask what piano and maths have to do with each other. She answers:

> Il piano l'ha scelto mia madre, [the piano, that my mother chose] matematica l'ho scelta io. [maths, that I chose]

which the Italian subtitles *normalize* into "Mia madre ha scelto il piano, io matematica" ['my mother chose the piano, I chose maths'].

Why did the subtitler choose to change the original sentences? L1 students usually admit that they would probably *say* the first sentence, while some of those more sensitive to language add that they would rather *write* the version reported in the subtitles, typically with the motivation that it sounds *more correct*. The slight redundancy induced by the topic-comment structure seems to be perceived as a less authoritative form. I will come back to the issue after examining another mismatch between the oral and the written language.

At a later point in the same film the protagonist – whose wife has become a terrorist and whose brother has committed suicide – accuses himself for not having been able to stop them. He explains, "I thought that everybody has the right to live as he or she wishes" and concludes

> Ma che libertà è morire? [but what kind of freedom is it to die?]

In the subtitles, the conjunction *ma* [but] at the beginning of the sentence disappears. Why?

FRANCESCO CAVIGLIA

Strange as it may appear to proficient native and non-native speakers and writers of Italian, some old tradition seems to dictate that a (written) sentence should not begin with a conjunction. This bizarre rule, of which I do not know the origin, has even made it into the syntax and style checker included with *Microsoft Word* (at least until version 2003), which warns the writer that "It is not advisable to start a sentence with a conjunction", despite plenty of evidence of the contrary in literature and journalism and despite the different opinion held by the highest authority on the Italian language.[3] I cannot claim with certainty that this phantom rule is the only reason why conjunctions at the beginning of sentences tend to drop from subtitles – a frequent choice made by the subtitlers of both *La meglio gioventù* and *L'ultimo bacio* – since dropping conjunctions also makes subtitles slightly more compact.

I suspect, however, that a deeper rationale was at work, maybe unconsciously to the subtitlers themselves. Here the subtitles reveal a hostile attitude to the traits of language perceived as pertaining to the *spoken* language.[4] Both the topic-comment structure and the use of a conjunction at the start of a sentence are loaded with instruction for the listener about the subject to be further illustrated in the rest of the sentence as well as the *attitude* of the forthcoming sentence to what has just been said. In other words, both are traits with a strong *instructional* (Weinrich 1976) and *dialogic* (Nølke 2002) value, i.e. traits which are crucial to real-time interaction of people in conversation.

For historical and cultural reasons, which are beyond the scope of this paper (but not of classroom intervention, hopefully), *oral* traits of language in Italian are often perceived as less valued than *written* traits, although strong variation is also to be found *within* the written code. However, the examples we just examined provide a rare opportunity of examining two variants of sentences with identical meaning and comparing their clarity and effectiveness. Not surprisingly, once the teacher ensures that both solutions are correct and stylistically acceptable, the students usually have no doubt choosing the *oral* solution as the more appropriate.

For both L1 and advanced L2 students, discussing and producing intralingual subtitles is a way of moving from passively adhering to what is perceived as 'standard' towards a more responsible attitude to language choices.[5]

3. SUMMARY: WHAT DID WE FIND OUT?

The examples and questions described above put the students into the role of language researchers, and allowed them to manipulate language in the process. The students themselves were often surprised by their own understanding of communication and usually appreciated the activities, with L1 secondary school students more inclined to discuss competing language solutions and L2 university students more inclined to theoretical aspects, as one might expect.

At the same time, the proposed activities did not constitute by any means a curriculum in language awareness. A simple list, rather than a structured table of contents, captured a few elements which I considered to have been *digested* by the students as a result of those activities:

1. dialogue constructs not only representations, but also relationships and identities, and is a means "to get things done";
2. understanding communication also requires noticing and giving a name to non-verbal elements, which may require borrowing categories from anthropology (e.g. *face work*);
3. the code (oral or written) does play a role in discussing *equivalence* in translation and even within the same language (e.g., in intra-lingual subtitles);
4. the oral code is not less valuable than the written one; actually, the written code can capture only a portion of the information conveyed by the spoken word;
5. in Italian, the written and the oral code are wide apart, with the written one traditionally perceived as superior; however, well-designed oral language (e.g. in film dialogue) can suggest solutions which are stylistically superior to those that are perceived as standard for the written code.

It is necessary to underline that the units described in this paper are far from representing a full-fledged curriculum in language awareness. Moreover, all these topics might also be examined in classrooms using other approaches and tools.

However, this paper suggests that dialogue in film – with or without subtitles – may deserve further consideration as a resource for language education, given both the quality of the language and the technical possibility of examining it at close range. The possibility of *manipulating*

FRANCESCO CAVIGLIA

the language by writing alternative subtitles adds yet another promising perspective, which I am currently exploring with L1 students.

NOTES

1 In the original English script, the teenagers speak in what I perceive as a (realistically) mildly-to-intermediate vulgar language. The Italian subtitles usually translate all swearwords, with the result of printing on the screen an extremely rude and offensive Italian language which many teachers and parents would not tolerate. The version dubbed into Italian chooses instead the language Italian teenagers (of a recent past) would use in similar circumstances: a few swearwords, but not necessarily in the same sentences as in the original; the spoken Italian is therefore far more faithful in register to the original than the subtitles. The DVD contains alternative soundtracks in German, French, Spanish and Italian, and subtitles in 20 languages.

2 Film dubbing and subtitling is already recognized as a valuable practice for advanced university students in L2 and translation studies (Taylor 1996). My point is that secondary school students too can have a say on questions concerning equivalence in language.

3 The website of the Accademia della Crusca argues for the use of conjunctions at the beginning of sentences in a section offering answers to frequently asked questions about the Italian language: http: //www. accademiadellacrusca.it/faq/faq_risp.php?id=3948&ctg_id=93, seen 2.2.2005.

4 The topic-comment structure is generally recognized as more frequent in spoken Italian (Berruto 1993: 48).

5 Not to speak of the choices *teachers* should make. The oral/written gap is not as evident in Italian as in French – for example, in Italian there are not two different morphological systems for oral and written language – but Andersen's (2002) suggestion to teachers and curricula makers for French of taking a position on *which language* should be prioritized at a given level deserves to be considered for Italian too.

BIBLIOGRAPHY

Andersen, H.L. 2002. 'Fransk tale og fransk skrift: Skal man undervise i to sprog på én gang?' In: C. Bache, M. Birkelund & N. Nørgaard (eds.), *Ny forskning i grammatik. Fællespublikation 10. Christianmindesymposiet.* Odense: Syddansk Universitetsforlag, 5-24.

Bakhtin, M. 1986. 'The problem of speech genre'. In: C. Emerson & M. Holquist (eds.), *Speech Genre and Other Essays*, translated by V.W. McGee. Austin: University of Texas Press, 60-102.

Bereiter, C. & M. Scardamalia 1989. 'Intentional learning as a goal of instruction'. In: L.B. Resnick (ed.), *Knowing, learning, and instruction: Essays in honor of Robert Glaser.* Hillsdale, New Jersey: Erlbaum, 361-392.

Brown, P. & S.C. Levinson 1987. *Politeness: Some universals in language use.* Cambridge: Cambridge University Press.

Bialystock, E. 1993. 'Symbolic representation and attentional control in pragmatic competence'. In: G. Kasper & S. Blum-Kulka (eds.), *Interlanguage pragmatics*. Oxford: Oxford University Press, 43-57.

Card, L. 1998. '"Je vois ce que vous voulez dire": Un essay sur la notion de l'équivalence dans les soustitres de *37°2 le matin* et de *Au revoir les enfants*'. *Meta*, XLIII, 2, 205-219.
Online at http://www.erudit.org/revue/meta/1998/v43/n2/, seen 3.2.2005.

Carter, R. 2003. 'Key concepts in ELT: language awareness'. *ELT Journal*, 57/1, 64-65.

Caviglia, F. 2004. 'Advanced literacy. Bridging traditions in the study of language and culture'. In: H. Lauge Hansen (ed.), *Foreign Language Studies and Interdisciplinarity*. Copenhagen: Museum Tusculanum Press, 105-120.

de Linde, Z. 1995. '"Read my lips": Subtitling principles, practices and problems'. *Perspectives: Studies in Translatology*, 3/1, 9-20.

Goffman, E. 1959. *The presentation of self in everyday life*. Garden City, NY: Doubleday.

Ivarsson, J. & C. Mary 1998. *Subtitling*. Simrishamm, Sweden: TransEdit HB.

Jung, U.O.H. 1990. 'The challenge of broadcast videotext to applied linguistics'. *IRAL: International Review of Applied Linguistics in Language Teaching*, 28/3, 201-221.

Kasper, G. & K.R. Rose 2002. *Pragmatic development in second language*. Malden, MA: Blackwell.

Kramsch, C. 1996. *Context and culture in language teaching*. Oxford: Oxford University Press.

Kovačič, I. 1996. 'Reinforcing or changing norms in subtitling'. In: C. Dollerup & V. Apel (eds.), *Teaching translation and interpreting 3: new horizons*. Papers from the Third Language International Conference, Elsinore, Denmark 9-11 June 1995. Amsterdam/Philadelphia: John Benjamins, 297-305.

Nornes, A.M. 1999. 'For an Abusive Subtitling (Subtitles of Motion Pictures)'. *Film Quarterly*, Spring 1999. Online at http://articles.findarticles.com/, seen 2.2.2005.

Nølke, H. 2002. 'La polyphonie comme théorie linguistique'. In: M. Carel (ed.), *Les facettes du dire. Hommage à Oswald Ducrot*. Paris: Kimé, 215-224.

Risager, K. 2003. *Det nationale dilemma i sprog- og kulturpædagogikken: et studie i forholdet mellem sprog og kultur*. Copenhagen: Akademisk Forlag.

Rossi, F. 1999a. *Le parole dello schermo. Analisi linguistica del parlato di sei film dal 1948 al 1957*. Roma: Bulzoni.

Rossi, F. 1999b. 'Doppiaggio e normalizzazione linguistica: principali caratteristiche semiologiche, pragmatiche e testuali del parlato postsincronizzato'. In: S. Patou-Patucchi (ed.), *L'italiano del doppiaggio*, Roma: Associazione Culturale "Beato Angelico" per il doppiaggio, 17-40.

Rossi, F. 2002. 'Il dialogo nel parlato filmico'. In: C. Bazzanella (ed.), *Sul dialogo. Contesti e forme di interazione verbale*. Milano: Guerini, 161-75.

Sabatini, F. 1985. 'L'italiano dell'uso medio: una realtà tra le varietà linguistiche italiane'. In: G. Holtus & E. Radtke (eds.), *Gesprochenes Italienisch in Geschichte und Gegenwart*, Tübingen: Narr, 154-184.

Tannen, D. 1992(1986). *This is not what I meant. How conversational style makes or breaks your relations with others*. London: Virago Press.

Tannen, D. 1989. *Talking voices: Repetition, dialogue and imagery in conversational discourse*. Cambridge: Cambridge University Press.

Tannen, D. 1992. 'How is conversation like literary discourse? The role of imagery and details in creating involvement'. In: P. Downing, S.D. Lima & M. Noonan (eds.), *The linguistics of literacy*. Amsterdam/Philadelphia: John Benjamins, 31-46.

Tannen, D. 1997. 'Involvement as dialogue: Linguistic theory and the relation between conversational and literary discourse'. In: M. Macovski (ed.), *Dialogue and critical discourse*. New York/Oxford: Oxford University Press, 137-157.

Todorov, T. 1984. *Mikhail Bakhtin: The dialogical principle*. Translation by W. Godzich. Minneapolis: University of Minnesota Press (Orig. edn. 1981, *Mikhail Bakhtine. Le principe dialogique*. Paris, Éditions du Seuil).

Weinrich, H. 1976. *Sprache in texten*. Stuttgard: Klett-Kotta.

Wildblood, A. 2002. 'A subtitle is not a translation: A day in the life of a subtitler'. *Language International*, 14, 2 (April), pp. 40-43. Online: http: //www.titelbild. de/Press_Reports/2002-04_Language_International/body_2002-04_language_ international.html

Quoted films

I soliti ignoti, by Dino Risi. Italy, 1956.

Lacombe Lucien, by Louis Malle. France, 1974. (The screenplay as book: Malle Louis & Patrick Modiano, 1974. *Lacombe Lucien*. Paris: Éditions Gallimard.

La meglio gioventù, by Marco Tullio Giordana. Italy, 2003.

L'ultimo bacio, by Gabriele Muccino, Italy, 2001. (The screenplay as book: Muccino, Gabriele & Mario Sesti, 2001. *L'ultimo bacio. La storia di tutte le storie d'amore*. Roma: Fandango. Also online: http: //www.kinematrix.net/articoli/ ultimo_bacio_sceneggiatura.htm, seen 2.2.2005).

Sliding doors, by Peter Howitt. UK, 1998.

Stand by me, by Rob Rainer. USA, 1986.

Appendix: A Technical Note
Sources of subtitled film dialogue

- DVDs;
- Teletext (to record subtitles, your video-recorder must have a 'record subtitles' or 'record teletext' function, which can be found on several recent VCRs or digital recorders);
- 'Close captioned' videocassettes (only available in some countries).

Reproducing a scene

DVDs offer quick access to scenes. Most DVD-players on computer have a 'bookmark' function which comes in handy for the teacher to prepare the scene to use in a presentation.

A freeware program, DVD Shrink (www.dvdshrink.org) can extract a scene from a DVD (or the whole DVD) onto a directory on the hard disk. A software DVD player (e.g. PowerDVD) can then open the directory and play its content as if it were a DVD. This procedure is legal at least in Sweden, as long as you have purchased the DVD and are not going to share the files with other people. In most other countries you simply may not 'rip' a DVD under any circumstances.

The rights to insert film scenes in a published work (e.g. on CD-ROM) cost about $500 per minute for Danish fiction and $1000 or more for Hollywood films (source: Systime A/S, Aarhus).

Sharing dialogues

It is illegal to share video files, so the only thing which can legally be shared is the timing of a scene (it can be read off from any DVD-player), followed by an explanation.

Some software players permit you to 'export' their bookmarks to a file.

Manipulating subtitles

Writing subtitles is a rewarding activity (read Wildblood, 2002 to get an idea of the process), although finding the right timing – the interval of time the subtitles are to stay on the screen – can be painful for a beginner. If subtitles in a language already exist, it is usually possible to adapt the timing of the existing subtitles to a new one.

Subtitle workshop (http: //www.urusoft.net/downloads.php), a freeware package, lets the user add subtitles to a video file and modify existing ones *available as text files*. Unfortunately, extracting the 'original' subtitles from a DVD is illegal in most countries. It may be possible, however, to obtain permission from the publisher for the purpose of writing subtitles in another language.

If someone has written alternative subtitles to a DVD and wants to share them with others, it is possible to distribute them with the help of a free computer program called *DVDSubber 2* (http: //www.darkwet. net/dvdsubber/News.asp), which permits adding external subtitles to a commercial DVD without actually modifying the DVD itself. *DVDSubber* is still 'work in progress' and building the distribution file requires some work. However, *using* external subtitles developed by others is easy (the DVD needs to be run on a computer).

Contributors

Hanne Leth Andersen
Associate Professor
Centre for Educational Development
University of Aarhus
Nobelparken
8000 Aarhus C
Denmark
E-mail: cfuhla@hum.au.dk

Francesco Caviglia
National Research Council – Institute for Educational Technology
Genova (Italy)
Via De Marini, 6
16149 Genova
Italy
E-mail: caviglia@itd.cnr.it

Claire Kramsch
Professor
Graduate School of Education
University of California,
Berkeley, USA
E-mail: ckramsch@berkeley.edu

Karen Lund
Associate Professor
Department of Educational Anthropology
The Danish University of Education
2400 Copenhagen NV
E-mail: karlund@dpu.dk

Karen Risager
Professor
Department of Language and Culture
Roskilde University
Roskilde
Denmark
E-mail: risager@ruc.dk

Eva Westin
Assistant Professor
Romance Institute
University of Lund
Lund
Sweden
E-mail: eva.westin@rom.lu.se